SOUL GUIDE ON PLANET EARTH

IVAN ANTIC

Translated by

Milica Breber

ISBN-13: 978-1978043947

TABLE OF CONTENTS

INTRODUCTION

A need for this kind of a reminder has been around for long, namely for some form of a guide that will enable human souls to remember who they are and why they are here. People know who they are, they have just forgotten it. Many bits and pieces of information of this kind are already in existence, but largely scattered and disorganized in various works and teachings, the old and the new ones, some are ideologically one-sided, some aim to be objective, but are incomplete, while a multitude of contemporary books on this topic merely stimulates the illusions and plants disinformation. Here we shall try to do what has not been done before, and that is to present the entire story in as objective way as possible.

Naturally, it will be coloured by the author's experience, my personal experience and maturity. It has both its good and bad sides. Bad sides are the personal limitations that I certainly do possess. The good side is that you can testify about this only from your own personal experience. One can speak about the life of a soul only through personal experience which has been percolated long enough to have achieved its ultimate objective value.

The good side in my case is the fact that during the past thirty years of my life I have made a serious effort to minimize my personal limitations and make the experience objective enough. This I have achieved by means of Zen Buddhist meditation *shikan-taza*, then with the countless out-of-body experiences, on the physical plain, in astral and ultimately in the realms above astral (hyperspace), as well as the experience of dying. Additional objectivity about the life of souls brought upon me the experience of meeting the souls of the dead and being acquainted with my spiritual guide. The nature of these experiences I have already explained about in my book *Sankhya*, related to the *Sankhya* teaching which is older than the *Vedas*, the teaching which objectively shows all categories of existence in all the dimensions. The chart of categories of *Sankhya* has shown itself to be the only totally objective and accurate map of everything that is going on, something I can use as an anchor and background to compare with my personal experiences in order to obtain objective value. For a better understanding of what

I am presenting here it will come in handy to read *Sankhya* as well. Furthermore, I have complemented my experiences and work on myself with the teaching of G.I. Gurdjieff, the ancient sufi knowledge and Gnosticism which he conveyed, and a good deal of material in this book will be based on these teachings.

Perhaps to a learned connoisseur of Buddhism, in particular Zen Buddhism, a question may arise as to why I mention the soul when it is not a very "Buddhist" thing to do. Indeed it is not, but the original teaching of Buddha together with the Zen Buddhism which best implements it do not negate the soul, they rather point to a much wider context than that of an individual soul and its experience. Buddhism does not negate the soul and the Divine, it is completely false. In his day, Buddha spoke of what happens with the souls during their life and after death, as well as the doings of the Divine. He merely stressed what it is that enables everything, the wider context of it all, and the practice of awakening, not the theoretical explanations, which had been covered well, back in his time. As an enlightened individual, Buddha knew too well that everything he uttered would become metaphysics, that the mind projects everything as an illusion, that the imagined has already taken place, that the description is solely that what is being described. Therefore he never spoke of the aim but only about the means of achieving the aim. He avoided, at all costs, the possibility of the aim becoming an object of religious worship before it was truly realized. And that is exactly what the unenlightened people always do: when they cannot achieve the spiritual goal through their own effort and transformation, they turn it into a religion in which they fantasize that the goal has already been achieved or will be achieved in some imaginary future, or that God has brought it himself. Buddha did not create a religion, he was only pointing towards the way of purification. He was the hygienist of suffering. His broader context is a lot more comprehensive for us today because the modern theory of The Universal Field[1] and the quantum holograph[2] deals with it in its own way, which is the foundation of

---

[1] See Gregg Braden's: *Divine Matrix* on the universal field in modern physics, as well as Lyn McTaggart: *The Field: The Quest for the Secret Force of the Universe.*

[2] On the holographic paradigm see Michael Talbot: *The Holographic Universe.*

reality, and according to which there is no difference between the supreme Divine reality, cosmos and our inner experience and the spiritual life. It is all one and the same happening; all of its processes, in its entirety, lead to the great awakening. This is the reason why Buddha spoke only of awakening, and why Buddhism is the teaching of awakening. For that reason it can be said that individual souls don't exist, for in the final outcome only the Absolute exists, and it is transcendental which means it cannot be defined – also there are individual souls who are basically the Absolute itself, its conscious subjects – because there is someone who is knowing the transcendental. If there were no souls, as the conscious subjects, that are capable of overcoming the body and mind, that are capable of understanding the inconsistency and the changeability of it all, there would be neither Buddhism nor awakening, nor Buddha himself. The question is only of the different depth of the insight, and the ways of observing one and the same thing.

The essence of awakening in Zen boils down to one saying: Know your face that you had had before you were born. It means: know your essence or soul that you were before you were incarnated into this body; that what you are in the absolute sense, independent of body and mind. That is the awakening. Only then the process of the individual experience of existing which we call the soul and its unity with the objective existence which we call the Absolute or the Divine becomes clear. It is one and the same process. Knowing that it is identical is awakening.

But awakening would not be what it is if the whole process of awakening were not understood, the whole life of an individual soul, the reason why there is the drama of life, and how it came to the awakening during its life in the physical body. We shall remind ourselves of that process here, although it is so painstaking and illusory that we would do better to forget it, like a nightmare we had had a long time ago. Maybe this is the way for us to help the dreaming souls to wake up without a start.

1. THE ORIGIN,

OR WHERE WE COME FROM

While describing the whole matter we must begin from the most general, and the most abstract explanation of the origin itself, in order to understand all the details of the life drama which souls have in this world.

In the foundation of all the existence is the Absolute or the Divine. Here we shall refer to it as the Divine Absolute. By doing so we shall avoid the theological deification of calling it only God, and the theoretical abstraction of calling it only the Absolute.

The Divine Absolute is uncreated, timeless, and with no boundaries, which means that it is all-pervasive and that nothing else exists outside of it. Since the language is always limited and one-sided, we can speak of it only in terms of the paradox: that it is everything, although it is none of it, that it cannot be known even though it lies in the foundation of every knowing, that it is a non-being although it forms the basis of every being, that it is nothing although it enables everything. In a nutshell, it is transcendental for the mind, or it is even above the mind.

The emanation first took place from the Divine Absolute together with the appearance of all the universes that exist, as well as the existence itself.

It must be described using the language of paradox. Hence, the Divine Absolute as such is always complete, therefore, nothing can emanate from it, because nothing is possible outside of it, it itself is nothing[3] - this is how much it is complete.

However, completeness as such cannot exist without the awareness of self. Unconscious completeness is not possible. On the other hand, paradoxal again, the completeness itself cannot be without the awareness of itself. Be as it may, the old Gnostic and Sufi myths say that the Divine (probably out of its own completeness) at one timeless moment became aware of itself and with this act split itself into itself and the conscious part.

---

[3] Buddhist teaching of emptiness, Apophatic theology, Cabalistic and Sufi teachings of the supreme Divinity speak of this, each in its own way.

That what it became aware of was itself, for nothing else exists nor can it be. But the act of becoming conscious like this made that what the Divine became conscious of seem like a projection, like something else. For every consciousness about something a projection, objectivization is needed, like for every painting the canvass is needed, and like for every shape a substance is needed or the material with which it is shaped. Objectivization is needed for the objective consciousness.

It is with this very act of the absolute consciousness of itself that all the existing world came into being or the objective universe with all of its dimensions and proportions.

All of the objective or the appearing universe is merely the basis that enables the reflexion of the Divine consciousness of itself, which is also the consequence of the act of the consciousness itself.

It is known as the undifferentiated Field[4] of all the possibilities, the root of all cause or the universal quantum Field, the Divine Matrix, The Quantum Holograph, it is called Nature or *prakrti* in the teaching of *Sankhya*.

Having seen itself[5] as a reflexion in this Field of consciousness the Divine began giving names and shapes. This is how the Divine acquired the first thought of itself as "I am".

And that is how the first trinity was born:
1. The Conscious Subject
2. The Object the Subject is aware of
3. The Process of Observing Both the Subject and the Object

In antiquity it was presented as:
1. The Divine as the Father (in Gnostic teachings – *purusha* in *sankhya*),
2. The all known existence as the Mother (*pleroma* in Gnosticism, the nature or *prakrti* in *sankhya*), and

---

[4] The definition of "The Field" in quantum physics is that it presents an invisible force which affects the creation of all the visible physical world, and that in this world everything that is divided in the physical world is connected in this field.

[5] Having seen as a reflection means: to observe one's image in the mirror, but to look into a part of one's self (without a mirror), to compare, to consider, to experience, to try, to measure one's own capability.

3. The objective consciousness of oneself, of existence, as the Son of God (in Gnosticism, in *sankhya mahat buddhi*, the first category of *prakrti*).[6]

The third one contains in itself the entire original trinity.

From the third one came into being everything that exists.[7]

Everything that exists carries in itself the nature of the original dualism (1 and 2), the dialectics of opposites, *yin* and *yang*, because based on the original dualism the third one was created along with everything else that came out of it.

Everything that exists is also an illusion or imagination of the Divine Absolute, because nothing can be outside of it. It all takes place within itself. Therefore, everything that seemingly displays itself as existence has two characteristics:

The first: All that is displayed is Divine in accordance with the holographic model, where every piece of a whole (the image) contains and mimics the whole (the whole image). The holographic model defines the obvious fact of how at the same time the universe, all that is created, and its unity exist, how it is all one although it may appear as the multitude.

The second: Since nothing is possible outside the Divine, it is only the emptiness (*sunyata*), everything emanates from it in the form of an illusion of the Divine or its dream of existence. The one who exists has no need to acknowledge it to itself. A need for such an acknowledgement arises only when it forgets itself. This is why everything that is created is merely implementation and materialization of this illusion.[8] Oblivion of itself as the Divine is the

---

[6] In Cabala only the Divine is called *ain*, emptiness or pure spirit; its first reflexion *ain sof*, The Infinite, universal Field; the third as the source of manifestation of all is called *ain sof aur*, the infinite uncreated light. Thus the nature of the supreme One is triple. *Ain* is limited with *ain sof*, and *ain sof* with *ain sof aur*. Further emanation of the Divine means more and more limitations of the lower spheres, all the way down to the rough material world.

[7] Tao Te Ching 42: *From Tao comes One; from One comes two; from two come three; those three give birth to all things. All things carry yin and yang. Through the union of these three vital energies they achieve unity.*

[8] Another way to present this same thing was done in Indian philosophy with the metaphor of the Divine dance, *Lila*, God is the dancer and his dance is the manifested world. Dance is neither separated nor different from the dancer, dance exists only while the dancer is dancing. Such manifested world is not different from God, even though it is perceived differently. We see it only when

materialization of the unconscious, or unconscious materialization. That is to say, materialization of the objective universe is a direct consequence of the oblivion of the Divine, the oblivion of itself, the implementation of this oblivion. But the implementation itself and the materialization of the unconsciousness assist the consciousness and self-realization, therefore, it is not a futile endeavour of moving in vain, endlessly.

A similar process takes place within the man, because man is a microcosm and his soul is the spitting image of the Divine: when a man forgets himself and falls into a dream, or an illusion, as a consequence of that the dreams, illusions, become the only reality.

This is why the answer to this paradox - why the act of itself caused the unconscious projection of the universe - man can achieve only with his own awakening - for only in a man's awakening the Divine Absolute keeps returning to itself.

Therefore the consciousness of itself has a dual nature: it is the highest affirmation of the very existence and at the same time the beginning of the illusion of existence.

All the real spiritual traditions describe the creation of the world as a fall into a deeper and deeper state of materiality and unconsciousness.

That is the reason why with the awakening a man rises and releases himself from all the illusions of materiality and unconsciousness. [9]

This Trinity, or the law of number three, shows how creation by itself happens. This is why the following process of creating anything has three forces: active, passive and neutral. The first is aspiration to do something, the second one is the resistance towards the aspiration in question, and the third one is the result. Those are the three *gunas* in *sankhya*. It is "The Holy Trinity" in esoteric Christianity.

---

he dances, as the manifested universe, while it is by itself transcendental and cannot be known. This same thing apophatic and cataphatic theology are trying to convey.

[9] According to this The Buddhist teaching of emptiness and awakening equals with the other teachings, with Cabala and esoteric Christianity, which teach that only the Divine is reality, and that the entire existing world is a consequence of the fall to the lower states and eclipses of the original consciousness – which can be retrieved only in man.

This was the process of initial creation itself that we have described here.

This process develops further, and expresses itself as everything that exists through the dimensions and proportions.

2. THE MANIFESTATION OF EVERYTHING THROUGH SEVEN PHASES OR PROPORTIONS

The process of creation further goes through seven phases or proportions. It is the law of number seven, which is known in the symbolism and mythology.

The process of further creation takes place according to the model of breaking up the holographic mirror into countless tiny bits and pieces, where each piece contains the whole.

In the very act of creating everything objective, which the Divine Absolute experienced as "I am", or "I exist", or "I am the existence itself", an independent thought of itself, the awareness of the very Divine existence separated, and an unstoppable aspiration to know all aspects of the Divine existence in all the possible shapes and emanations happened.

This independent Divine awareness of itself is known as "the first and the most beautiful angel of God", the light of consciousness which displays the very Divine as such.[10]

The direct experience of such original awareness of existence is the experience of unity with the existence itself.

This experience of unity automatically created the illusion that that consciousness was from the Divine existence itself.

This illusion made the illusory drive in the consciousness that it can create of its own accord, that it is the Divine itself, and not merely a reflection of it – Divine is always beyond the conscious-

---

[10] It is falsely interpreted in Judeo-Christian religion in the negative light as Lucifer, in order to conceal the true meaning, and to ensure that the Roman Christian Church separates from the gnostic myth, which testifies of this. The Gnostics were the first true Christians. The authorities of Rome persecuted them as the biggest enemies but could not suppress or destroy their religion. That is the reason why they made the Christian church in Rome so that Gnostics would not make it. They falsified the Gnostic gospels and The Bible we have today, and they falsified the whole mythology with the sole purpose of making it seem different from the original and true Christian faith, and concocted the church dogma we know today.

ness, and can be neither the object nor the contents of the awareness because it precedes and facilitates it. It is the consciousness
itself, not the consciousness about something.

According to the legend the first Son of God, the bearer of the
light of the consciousness and existence, all by himself created the
other worlds. With this act he turned himself into some kind of an
outcast because he imagined that he was the Divine itself, although
he was merely its reflection.

Since the newly created worlds were not God's original intent
or doing, *because the Divine never had a plan or intention to create any worlds*, they were being created from this estranged Divine
consciousness in a rougher and rougher form as bigger and bigger
illusions. In other words, *God is so whole and complete that it is
impossible for him to create a world of any kind*. He is, as an Absolute, everything that can exist and nothing exists outside of it. If
you want to be serious in your faith in God, you shouldn't imagine
that God created the world. We can speak of the manifested or the
"created" world only as an illusion (*Maya*). The Divine being the
only reality, as a freedom of all the possibilities, now means that
the illusion is real. That is the reason why we can speak of it. That
is why we live in it. That is why awakening from the illusion is
real. The final solution to these paradoxes comes only through the
transcendence of the mind, because only in the mind illusion can
be made and illusion can be eliminated. Later we shall concentrate
on this practice.

We are aware of the seven proportions of creation which we
shall describe here.

Since the universe is a creation of the Divine consciousness of
itself, it has kept some of the important characteristics of the Divine Absolute down to the lowest proportion and the roughest dimension of the material universe. Those are the characteristics of
the holographic unity and the freedom of all the possibilities.

In this manner the objective universe emanated together with
the Divine consciousness of itself as "I am", and became The Field
of free manifestation of all the possible emanations and events,
everything that is possible of existing and taking place in any way,
shape or form that already exists as potential in the universal Field
(*prakrti*), all at once, timeless or outside the realms of time. All of
it was created in the first act of the reflection – because with this

act the Absolute itself was reflected. But only as the potential. That is why there is nothing new. Everything that can exist and happen was created with the first act of the existence, but it remained potential. To a subjective observer, who is limited with his own space and circumstances, something that was potential becomes real, and then he sees it as something "new". "New" exists only in the subjective experience of the observer, because of his limited focal point. Conscious subject chooses possibilities one by one from the endless ocean of possibilities and brings them to life. In the course of revealing something new he has the illusion of the passing of time, for not all the possibilities are manifested at the same time, something "happens" before, and something after. *The important thing to remember here is that the conscious subject is the key player, the one who turns possibilities into existence, who transforms the potential into something real, and in this way creates an existence*.

This is the reason why this is the universe of free will, of manifesting freely everything that can be manifested.

Together with this everything is bound in unity, but according to the model of the fragmented holograph, where every part contains the whole picture. This is possible because of the timeless omnipresence of everything created.

Breaking up the mirror of the holistic whole of the Divine was happening in a progressive way in seven phases. Those phases develop in way of spiral motion (by breaking up the Divine holograph) and circulating from the higher proportion to the lower. In the same way the consciousness of existence declines to lower and lower states. Every proportion obtains consciousness of itself and it automatically repeats the original illusion that it is self-sufficient and then creates the lower proportion, in which the consciousness is more conditioned.

1   The Absolute as a whole and the Divine itself. It enables all of the timeless space that facilitates everything else. It is the pure being that precedes the consciousness of the Self.

2   All the galaxies. They have above themselves only the space itself that contains them. That is the consciousness of the Self as the space and the context of all the happening.

3　All the stars. It is the implemented consciousness, in all its shapes in which it possibly could exist. It is manifested as the light of the stars.

4　Our star, The Sun. The consciousness of the lives of the human souls on Earth is there.

5　Planetary systems around the Sun. There is the consciousness of all the aspects of action and the dynamics of experience of the human souls on Earth.

6　The Earth and the organic world on it. There the consciousness is identified with the physical life in an individual body, plants and animals alike.

7　Moon as the satellite of the Earth. There the consciousness is in the state of sleep or obsession which is a result of the complete identification with the body.

This progressive growth we had to observe in this manner, from our perspective, here from the Earth, because we cannot observe it from some other imaginary point. This is how it affects us, and this is how we must observe. The growth would be the same from some other observation point, the differences would depend merely on the proportion from which the observation is taking place.

Those are the proportions of existence. Each and every one has its own logic and therefore cannot be interfered with. The nature of every existence can only be understood in the context of the proportion to which it belongs. The higher proportion affects the lower, whereas every lower one uses the higher for "food". For example, the Moon feeds on all organic life on Earth and attracts the energy of all the living beings. Even though it is on a lower scale from that of the Earth, it, with its gravitational pull, attracts all of the happening of the organic world. If the Moon suddenly stopped or disappeared, all of the life on Earth would stop. Moon affects the organic world like the pendulum on the clock which with its movement generates the motion of the clock mechanism, the organic life. Quite naturally, all planets of the solar system manage organic life, but the Moon is the most influential because it is the closest to us, and because with it ends the spiral of proportion in our direction. Similarly, the Earth uses the influences of other planets in the solar system, the solar system which is under the influence of the galaxy etc.

Moon is a big electromagnet which with its motion induces the life energy on Earth. This induced life energy is all organic life. All celestial bodies are electromagnets that with their own motion induce all the life that exists in the universe.

A combination of cosmological theories of the Electric and the Holographic universe, as well as the Strong Anthropic Principle (SAP) is the truest to reality.

In every proportion the Divine divides itself over and over again, and forms the Divine of that particular proportion, once again in accordance with the holographic model, into smaller entities. This is how the Divine exists and rules all the galaxies, together with all the stars and all their planetary systems, as well as one Divine entity that rules every planet on which there is organic life.

The Divine consciousness further divides itself into every conscious being that exists in all the worlds.

A certain number of laws rule every proportion which impose a set of conditions upon the proportion.

In the Absolute (1) rules only one law, the complete and utter state of unconditionality.

In all the galaxies (2) rule the three laws, those that in the Absolute itself were one, now have divided into three separate laws.

Six laws rule all the stars (3): three coming from the higher proportion and three that they themselves create by implementing the trinity.

The Sun (4) has twelve laws adding up: three forces that rule the worlds of the second class, six forces that rule over the worlds of the third class, and three forces of the Sun itself.

Planets (5) have twenty-four laws or forces that rule over them: addition of the preceding (3+6+12) and the three of its own laws which gives the total of 24.

The Earth is ruled by 48 forces or laws: the addition of all the preceding ones (3+6+12+24) and the three of its own laws which take place due to the force of trinity. [11]

---

[11] This description of seven proportions is taken from the Peter Ouspenski's book *"The Cosmological Lectures"*

The Moon is ruled over by 96 laws.[12]

If the Moon had a satellite, it would have 192 laws, and so forth.

In this way every lower plain is more conditioned and more dense. The Will of the Divine Absolute directly affects only the second proportion, the third one is already conditioned by the trinity, and all the lower ones are more and more conditioned by the greater number of the laws and forces.

This should explain why life on Earth is the way it is, hard and conditioned. The Earth is pretty far away from The God's source and the unconditionality.

---

[12] We can observe here that the proportions of manifesting the universe largely correspond with The Fibonacci sequence, and maybe it is one and the same thing. It is a mathematical sequence in many physical, chemical and biological instances. It was named after the Italian mathematician Fibonacci. It represents a sequence of numbers where the two preceding numbers give the value of the following member of the sequence. According to the same principle the anatomic structure of the human body exists.

3. MANIFESTATION OF EVERYTHING THROUGH FIVE DIMENSIONS

The entire manifestation of the universe consists of different frequencies or vibrations. The expansion of the frequencies has its own universal regulation, which is, in the ancient teachings conveyed to us by G.I. Gurdjieff, called The Laws of Octaves. In brief, from the initial to the frequency double in size, there are seven phases of their augmentation. This period of doubling the vibrations is called an octave, in the course of which the eighth part represents doubled first frequency and the start of a new octave. The growth process itself takes place in seven phases. This is why we have seven tones, seven colours of the rainbow, seven phases in the crystal formation, etc. Due to the holographic model of the universe, the law of number seven is shown in all the processes of creation, not only in the proportions we have previously described.

If we depict this law with a line of growing vibrations from A to B which is double in size (A------B), the whole process will have two breaking points where the vibrations keep slowing down. The first one is more likely to be in the beginning, and the second one somewhere near the end (A---1-----2-B). These two moments have a tendency to change the direction of the vibrations, so that it never develops in quite the same way. That is why you can never find straight lines or anything identical in nature. The first breaking point will turn the line once, and then the other moment of slowing down will turn the line for the second time before the vibrations are doubled. The new process of doubling, a new octave will turn the line of the growing vibrations and this is how spirals are made, from the DNA to the spirals of the galaxies. Thus, universe manifests itself into a multitude of shapes and forms that are never the same.

Because of these breaking points no process of realization can go directly to the aim, without any obstacles and additional investing of energy. We know this from our personal experience when we start something then the work changes, gets harder, gets lazy and then it turns into something different, we need to apply ourselves assiduously in order to continue in the planned direction towards our aim. Unless we give ourselves the additional boost of energy, it will continue in the new direction unnoticed, we will falsely think that we are moving towards our aim. The work, following the first breaking point spontaneously moved in the new direction, while we think we are moving towards our goal. Only by means of an objective observation from the side one can see that we have changed and are doing something else, or we are aware of it but find ways of justifying it to ourselves and rationalizing it. This is the same principle like in spreading some idea, for example, where from the initial point it becomes a twisted dogma and something completely different, but the followers of this idea still believe they are holding on to the initial goal, convinced in their reasons and justification. Their new interpretations and insisting on the dogma only represent the justification of turning. A good example of this difference and unconscious turning are the founders of great religions, and what their followers today are. The total opposite or a bad imitation.

In order for any process of realization to reach the end successfully, one must be aware of these two phases of slowing down and turning, and additional energy must be put in for the process to remain on course.

Because of the breaking phases of manifestation comes the versatility of the emanation. As their frequencies constantly crisscross different dimensions of manifested universe are created. We can see them as vibrations of different density or quality. There are five of them, and in antiquity they were represented symbolically as the five elements: Earth, Water, Fire, Air and Ether.

All the proportions of the universe with spiral interference and interconnecting are emanated through these five dimensions.

1 Firstly they exist as the consciousness itself. It is emanated as the space in which everything else can be emanated. That is the element of Ether. The universal quantum Field of all the possibilities.

2 Then the consciousness forms itself into the notions and abstract ideas. That is the element of Air. The highest frequency of the manifested universe. That what the consciousness is aware of, abstract and invisible like the air itself, but can be noticed and puts things in action. The consciousness takes shape of a thought here.

3 Ideas need to be moved, developed, formed and joined together. This stimulating will for developing certain ideas is presented with the element of Fire, which is visible and efficient, but without a specific shape. The will or energy joins the consciousness and thought here.

4 Different aspects of ideas need to be looked into and crystallised in one specific resulting shape. The power of separating one shape from the multitude that precedes it is represented with the element of Water. Water is visible and has shape, not its own rather the idea which it represents, the dish that holds it in. The consciousness shaped into a thought with energy here gets its first concrete form, the prototype.

5 Realisation of a specific form and its materialisation which is represented by the element of Earth.

In the process of crisscrossing the frequencies of all the proportions rules the law of causality, for it is spontaneous and unconscious, however because of the spontaneity and unconsciousness, it contains the law of accidentality. Therefore, both laws exist side by side, the law of causality as well as the law of accidentality. This is the reason why there are processes which cannot be foreseen with pure mathematical precision, processes that can only be partially predicted with higher or lesser degree of accuracy, and the processes that cannot be predicted, at all. The causality exists because of the force of the emanation, and accidentality because of the very freedom of the manifestation of everything. Both are based on the unconsciousness of the manifestation itself. Both must exist together. If the causality were the only factor, nothing new would come about, one and the same thing would be repeating itself into oblivion, and if the accidentality were the only factor nothing meaningful would ever take shape, nor would the manifestation itself make any sense.

4. HUMAN BODY IS THE OUTCOME OF THE MANIFESTATION OF ALL THE PROPORTIONS AND DIMENSIONS

The manifestation of all the proportions and dimensions is finalized in the shaping of the human body.

This is the reason why the human body is a microcosm. The holographic nature of the universe according to which every particle mimics the whole, enables it.

The man's body, as the outcome of creation and the entire manifestation contains all the dimensions and the proportions of the universe. All the dimensions are within the man not outside of him. This is the key thing to be considered while contemplating on the higher worlds and dimensions, so that they would not be sought after outside the man in vain. The key thing of a man's realisation and awakening is the knowing that everything is within him, and not outside of him. The man is as unconscious as the degree to which he keeps looking for his outcome on the outside, and the degree to which he is dependent on the external influences.

The pure *consciousness* of the self (Ether) can reside only in him; the highest vibrations of actions as ideas or *thoughts* (Air); *the will* and the capacity to exchange ideas and transform them (Fire); The ability to *feel* the nature of various ideas and states, in order to be able to choose and modify the true ones, the ones that represent their outcome (Water); The ability for them to be materialized, to be given a concrete shape (Earth).

Therefore, only in a man's body the universe can implement the consciousness (Ether), to think about himself (Air), to express the will for action and the realization of ideas (Fire), to feel how he should work (Water) and to realize it (Earth).[13]

---

[13] This is the formula of the Divine creation that Cabala refers to as the *tetragrammaton*, the name of God, JHVH. The biggest secret of the Cabala is that the *tetragrammaton* is in a man, that man is *tetragrammaton* – a process through which God creates. The secret is revealed here for you. In Judeo-Christian religions it is concealed with the story of the outer God.

This process of realization manifests itself through proportions, and they are also placed in the human body. Those are the modules of being that are commonly known as the seven centres, or the seven levels of consciousness, or the seven *chakras*. Those are all the ways of existence in which a man can exist, from the lowest sensual and material, to the highest the Divine.

Due to the spiral nature of the emanation, that takes place because of those two breaking points, every way of existing is more or less modified from the original Divine. Thus, the highest is the least modified and the closest to the awareness of itself, and the lowest one is the furthest away from the consciousness and the most conditioned. The lowest chakra is represented by the Moon, as well as the manifestation of the proportions.

When this type of the manifestation of the universe ended according to the principles of the holograph and free will of all the possibilities, it finalized in the individual consciousness of the self, the ultimate reflection of God's consciousness of himself, in the man as the man's consciousness "I am". Hence, man is a microcosm, that is to say the finalization of the shaping of the cosmos, man is a holograph where the meaning of all the dimensions and proportions are defined. The entire universe is within the man, not on the outside. The entire universe man finds within himself, by working on himself through his own effort and transformation in order to become the pure conscious subject of the objective existence. By purifying himself and entering the higher spheres of consciousness the man perfects the outside world as well. This is the reason why any man's knowing and transforming the outside world only, without the corresponding inner realization and transformation, can cause havoc and destruction.

All true teachings convey this very message when they tell us that man was born at the end of creation, that man was born perfect, as the crown of God's creation, and that he was born in the image of God.

5. THE DUAL NATURE OF THE EMANATION OF GOD: THE OBLIVION AND THE AWAKENING

In order to understand that the universe is in the man as well as on the outside of him, besides the holographic model, it is imperative that we comprehend the dual nature of the emanation of the Divine Absolute in the manifested universe.

The first one informs us that the manifestation of the universe is the ultimate decline into the oblivion of oneself and unconsciousness, and the second one is the process of awakening and self-realization. Those two processes are identical although seemingly they appear opposed. All the manifested world is based on the illusion of those two opposing sides.

As the proportions go down to the lower levels of existence, into a more inferior and rougher dimension, the original consciousness twists more and more into an illusion.

Actually, the entire manifestation through proportions and dimensions is nothing but the decline of the Divine consciousness into bigger and bigger conditionality, into the bigger oblivion of oneself.

This oblivion keeps materializing as something on the outside, as something different from the Divine, as we have stated before. To the Divine consciousness itself no materialization or the manifestation is needed, because it is already what it is, the reality itself, or the reality in itself. For this reason every manifested world can exist only as an illusion and unconsciousness. That is why the act of materialization itself exists, as the act of maintaining the unconsciousness and oblivion which, in this instance, is the act of reminding us of the oblivion, the materialization of oblivion which with its own objectivisation reminds us of this very oblivion and leads us to the awakening. All of the manifested universe is merely a reflexion of the oblivion or unconsciousness which at the same time is the act of awakening itself. In the pure consciousness of itself, the world as objective reality disappears.

The unconscious illusion as the objectivisation of the world never ends on the outside, but always in the man, as his awakening. It macrocosmically manifests itself as all the created world, and microcosmically as the Man's unconsciousness. Man was created to experience enlightenment, so that the illusion of estranged existence could end, the illusion that anything could exist outside the Divine Absolute.

Both of these acts, falling into oblivion as the manifestation of the universe, and awakening because of this very act of manifestation, are expressed as God's *existence*.

Therefore, only *existence* exists, as the Divine Absolute, there is no nothingness.

Therefore, the nature of the Divine is shown only here and now.

The nature of the consciousness of itself is, likewise, revealed only here and now.

Therefore, the consciousness of itself is no different from the existence of here and now.

Therefore, the nature of the consciousness of itself possesses the supreme consciousness and the understanding of the existence, for it is no different from the existence itself.

Therefore, nothing in reality was emanated from The Divine Absolute, it is itself all the time, here and now, for nothing else can be. That is why when we say that all that illusory emanation finalises into the image of man, it means that the outer universe is actually in him. It is just a different way of saying that the man is a microcosm. For the same reason we speak of the emptiness (*sunyata*) as the essence of everything manifested, of the numbness of the illusion *(nirvana)* as the awakening. It is merely an alternative way of expressing that nothing is manifested only the Divine Absolute is. If it is defined as empty, because if we name it we objectivize it, then we lose its very presence of here and now, as the consciousness of self, thus projecting it as some illusion. The Nothingness of the Absolute refers to annihilation of its names and shapes, not of itself, because nothing can refer to it.

For the same reason the Devine cannot be known in any other as way as anything but the awareness of oneself, the man, as the outcome of everything manifested. Consequently, for the most supreme and final knowing and realisation only numbness is needed, the quietening down of all the shaping and projections.

6. ORGANIC LIFE AS THE FOUNDATION
OF THE HUMAN BODY

If human body was created at the end of all creation, as the crown or the outcome of all the previous processes of emanation, it was not instantly created. It is a result of a long term shaping of the universe into finer, more perfect and more meaningful forms.

All organic world and life originated as the transition from the very simple shaping and emanating of proportions through the dimensions, towards giving meaning to it all, to the awakening in every single shape and life form.

If the whole process of manifestation can be presented as the reflection of the consciousness of itself, then the organic world and life present the polishing of the mirror in which the one who is, the consciousness of itself reflects itself.

Inorganic world is manifested through the mathematical rules of proportions and dimensions. This is the reason why its versatility is made up of a certain number of atom and molecule combinations, crisscrossing their frequencies. It is the type of a rough surface on which no reflecting is possible. Organic life and world are the formation of a superior kind, leading and defining towards the universal meaning of life. This defining is like polishing a surface which should become crystallized enough in the universal sense so that it can reflect that what exists.

Organic world is not possible on higher proportions than that of the Earth. Or on the lowest one, on which the Moon resides. ***Completely developed organic life is always possible in the form of a thin layer on the surfaces of the planets that have their own satellites***. The reason for this is – there have to be other celestial bodies near the planet that will, with their own magnetic induction initiate the complexity of forming of the elements into a higher order of the one spontaneously taking place with the manifestation of proportions and dimensions, in organic order.

The same thing happens in the very emanation of the Divine in seven phases or proportions, which can be seen in the example of increasing the frequency from A, to double value, B, where two transitions of the phase can be observed, one at the beginning, another at the end of the process (A----1-----2-B). So the first transition happened immediately after the appearance of the consciousness of itself in the Divine Absolute (A), it manifested as the inorganic world, and the second transitional phase took place at the end of the manifestation of proportions, as the organic life on Earth, during the previous phase, before the Moon (B).

The process of perfecting the experience of being in the organic world has been emanating by creating the organic life forms with assorted organs of sense and action. Those are different abilities of perception and activity. All living beings are divided simply into the number of sense and action organs they possess. From the simplest microorganisms with one sense only, to a multitude of beings with different combinations, to the only one being with all the eleven organs, which is the man. The eleven organs of perception and action are: five senses – hearing, sight, touch, taste and smell, and the five action organs are – tongue, legs, arms, the organs of excrement and the sexual organs. The eleventh organ is the mind, reason, the organ of thought, it summarizes and designs perception and the activity of all the other organs. That is why it is placed in the brain from where it manages the entire body.

According to the genealogy of the organisms on Earth there is an obvious link between the ability of movement and sensory perception, and intelligence. From the unicellular organisms, plants and animals, to the division of the animal kingdom into arthropods, mollusks, echinoderms and the vertebrates, to the mammals, we can see clearly that the number of sense and action organs, which enable better movement and perception, and consequently larger involvement in the events, enables proportionately higher intelligence.

Parallel with the appearance of the organic world on the physical plain, on Earth, that is the element of earth, nature shaped the entities with the ability of perception and action in the higher dimensions, as well. It happened because nature in all its dimensions is one big information field in which every event that repeats itself forms a morphogenetic field[14] and becomes an independent entity.

---

[14] On morphogenesis and morphogenetic fields see the works of Rupert

Everything is shaped by the event. On the physical level it is apparent in the fact that elements and particles join together by attracting and acting together into a new, wider whole, the symbiosis of some body, some planet or the galaxy itself. On the plains higher than the physical world, in astral, the same thing happens with the energy of the impressions and emotions, which also have their frequencies. That is why astral is full of entities that live on taking someone's energy, especially the type of energy which happens through emotional discharge.

In short, parallel with shaping the organic living beings, on the physical plain, nature shaped inorganic beings, independent entities on higher plains, mostly in astral (the element of water), which is right above the physical plain and the element Earth. In the tradition they are known as the elementals of nature, inorganic beings, spirits and demons. To humans they are mostly neutral entities that participate in nature's doings with its dimensions, but there are dangerous beings that feed off the energy created by the organic beings, and especially humans who possess the strongest, concentrated type of energy.

The entire nature is one huge information field which due to the very presence of consciousness turns into the material forms. The thought or the name is in the element of Air the synthesis of various forms of immediate sensory impressions on the physical plain, the element of Earth, or those earlier shaped by the informative action of the older morphogenetic field. No thought is new, it is just a more subtle reflection of a physical experience on the higher plains that connects the mind or the brain like a medium. Therefore, the name and shape, object and subject which determines it

---

Sheldrake. Briefly, this notion determines the origin of nature's forms, the pattern according to which every part of a living being is formed. There is no given information about the shape in the gene, what cell will become the arm cell, and which of the head. This is being decided by the field outside the organism, the subtle body, not physical, that exists like a mold that shapes the physical body. The fields of events and behavior of certain community are also present. That what keeps repeating itself becomes a subtle pattern on higher plains and it has a feedback effect on the behavior and shaping of the physical activities. This feedback effect of a formed field on the physical plain is called a *morphic resonance*.

are not different, they are forms of one and the same nature, but on different dimensions and proportions. The shape is more rough and material, and the name or thought higher, finer form of the same event. The idea in the element of the Air is the physical shape in the element of Earth. As the subtle version of the rough form, the thought is information about the rough form. When we see some thing, straight away we receive the thought that that is that thing. A thing became an idea in us. *The reverse process also takes place: ideas become things through us, they become real. Man's being turns ideas into manifested forms, and manifested forms takes back to the world of ideas and gives them meaning.*

In its lower dimensions the nature manifests itself as the rough form, in higher dimensions as energy, and in the highest and the most subtle dimensions the nature is just a vibration or information. A gathering of information about the nature's activities constitutes a man's mind. Brain is an organ fine enough that can absorb the frequencies of thought and maintain them, repeat and combine them. Thoughts are not in the brain, they are informative reflection of the field of some other experience. When we see a rough object, automatically a subtle vibration appears in us, the thought of this object. It is all the same nature: an object in a rough form is the thought of it in the fine informative form. It is the same phenomenon in two states, both as a shape and a thought. Only the illusion of time and space separates and distinguishes idea from shape.

By mental and sensory perception we refine rough objects into information of those objects. *In this way we return to a higher original state,* because before they ensued as rough objects, they existed in higher dimensions as information or ideas. Later they materialized as the rough objects. In such a way we bring them back to a higher, original state using perception. *With intellectual knowing and reason we finalize the process of organic creation and materialization. The process of creation is therefore always incomplete without the presence of a conscious subject. Everything manifested finds its outcome in the conscious subject.*

Gathering of those finest vibrations happens because of the power of attraction of the consciousness in man, his soul. *The presence of human soul itself in a man guides the nature to forming all organic life, informing itself, designing and estab-*

lishing in that body and through him everything that enables life and the culture of living. This designing is seen as the human civilization and technology.

The Divine Spirit or the Absolute projects all of its possibilities into matter, into a concrete shape, from the world of ideas to the world of concrete realization. *The perception of those shapes, which takes place in all living beings, and most complete in man, retrieves shape into the world of ideas, closes the circle, makes the Divine presence whole.* With the perception of objects and events we design them, that is, we turn them into ideas and with this we give them meaning. Using perception we return the manifested world into the world of ideas. And in doing so we make the process of creation and events complete.

What the Divine does on the macrocosmic plain, man with his perception finalizes on the microcosmic plain. Man with his act of awareness finalizes the work of the Divine. That is the work on the trans substantialization or deification (Greek: Θεωσις *teosis*, lat: deificatio) of the matter or the nature.

Human being is a transductor[15] that converts the Divine energy from lower to the higher shapes, to the consciousness and the sense of oneself. This conversion takes place through *chakras*.

All conscious beings who possess perception, plants and animals alike, participate in this work, not only the man, but only in man it reaches the level of completion and returns to Divine. The consciousness which returns to the Divine this way is enriched with experiences of all kinds. This enrichment of the experience of being through all the living species is in a certain way actualization of the consciousness of itself as the Divine Absolute.

---

[15] Transductor is a device which converts one type of energy into another. Conversion can be to / from electric, electro-mechanic, photonic, photovoltaic, or some other source of energy. While the term transductor is usually followed by sensor/detector, every device converting energy can be considered a transductor.

7. HUMAN BODY AS THE FOUNDATION
OF PERSONALITY

Plant and animal species simply gather impressions or experience of complexity of all aspects of the organic life on the level of elementary movement and survival. This gathering of the consciousness of rudimentary existence transfers from the simpler life forms on to more and more complex forms. When it reaches a certain "critical mass" of the complexity of experience, it becomes suitable to cross over into the human form, the form of a human body.

Gathering of the experience of existence on the levels lower than the human body is particular and linear. That was the compilation of possible impressions in the form of a mineral, microorganism, plants, fish, reptiles, mammals. It was based on simple forming and ways of survival.

Informative entity with which the existence (experience) in the roughest form is established is the one in the form of the mineral. That is the starting point of the evolution of elementary perception in the physical world. The very combination of composing elements is tested here and their characteristics in various combinations. Previously, it existed as an entity in the inorganic sphere, as the inorganic being or the elemental of nature. Every informative entity must cross from the inorganic to the organic sphere for only in the organic sphere, due to the three-dimensionality, the complete concretization of all of the experience of the existence from all of its dimensions – in the form of the mind. In the three-dimensional physical world perception keeps evolving further, from one incarnation to another, as a unicellular organism, then a multicellular in various forms, first as the partly immobile (plants), then more mobile (animals), in the evolutionary order which determines the ability of movement as the only way of gathering impressions (*samskara*) about the existence and the development of intelligence. As an arthropod, insect, mollusk, fish, amphibian, bird, mammal – until the impressions that can be gathered with simple movements and concern for the survival are completed, so that the process of physical individuation forms as a being which is the most competently equipped with all the sense organs, as well as the organs for action, to a degree that it is capable of using tools and instruments, and that being is the man.

The purpose of development of the process of physical individuation and perception is for the human shape to come into existence.

However, the process of the physical individuation is not complete then, either.

When it matures in the highest animal form, it is incarnated as the most primitive human form – and only then the process of *karma* begins. Those are mostly people from the "primitive communities" with tribal, national and religious identity very strongly expressed. It is displayed in the totem of the tribal community that represents the animal from which, according to the legend, its members originated from, as well as the belief that the souls of the dead go into animals, more specifically get incarnated as them. Outside such communities, the primitive human shape can be recognized in the visage and the general lifestyle which is focused on hard labor, and of numbness when it comes to consciousness and spirituality. Also, there can be physical and mental retardation (for example mongoloid people). Attachment of the primitive man to the impressions (*samskare*) is reflected in the level of conditionality of his instinctive behavior, and especially in the habits (in the thoughts, words and deeds), in his mechanicalness, and attachment to the tradition.

Only when it reaches the human body the process of individuation becomes the adequate residing place of the human soul – to the degree allowed by the Divine consciousness – for only the Divine which enables all gives essence to the human soul. Divine is the essence of man. Man's soul originates from the Divine, and not from nature. A man has a human soul only to an extent to which he receives, filters through himself and realizes the Divine that facilitates all. Before that only the informative entity exists as the principle of individuation of nature in the animal forms, but also in many human ones that are immature.

From the moment of existence in the human form the experience of living receives the spark of the Divine spirit, conse-

quently, in that body the reincarnation process of the human soul starts with the sole purpose of experiencing the being in all aspects, bringing it to consciousness and as such returning it to the Divine. Since man is a microcosm, this returning happens from within, in the man, as his way home to himself, The Self, pure consciousness freed of all objects and contents, and every illusion of individuality. That is the self-knowledge or God-knowledge in the human experience.

Since nothing is outside the Divine Absolute, the being that knows itself in the absolute sense, realizes the knowledge of the Divine in itself.

8. THE COMPLETE PERSONALITY AS THE FOUNDATION OF THE SOUL

When the process of individuation of the organic perception evolves through animal forms, it merely has the consciousness of the objects, not of itself. This is why animals cannot change themselves (they do not have an ego) nor correct their behavior, they have no choice and always follow what the circumstances and instincts decide.

While evolving through human forms, the process of individuation and perception has dual awareness, both of the objects and of the self, and all human evolution boils down to the transformation and perfecting of the subjects through the differentiation of the objects.

Human form is a transition from the animal to the Divine, that is to the spiritual. This is the reason why there are both the immature people who have a stronger attachment to the body, objects and the contents of their activities, and the mature ones who display a bigger independence from the body, psychological objectivity and individuality.

When finalizing its evolution through the human form, the process of individuation completely transcends the world of objects and realizes a triple consciousness: of objects, of the subject which is aware of the objects, and of the Divine Absolute which enables both the subject and the objective world.

The final forming of the personality as the image of the Divine can be found in the view that there is nothing but the Divine, and, additionally, the utter and complete submission to the Divine.

Therefore, the forming and the essence of the authentic personality of man is not of this world. Of this world can be the multitudes of I which share and condition the Man's personality. An authentic personality of man can be the image of what supersedes the body and the organic world in general, *the opening of man to infinity of the Divine that gives entirety to his whole personality.*

9. THE ORGANIC WORLD AS THE STAGE FOR THE DRAMA OF THE PERSONALITY

Experience of existence of the organic life in a human body unifies and designs in the sense of entirety, on a higher level of simple movement and survival: it turns into the drama of life, the trying out of all the possible *events and experiences* that shape the entire person. *Only as a person the experience of being can be returned to the Divine to meet its wholeness.* The man is the connecting factor of the fragmented holograph of the Divine Matrix according to which he was created, as his personification. A complete person is the personification of the Divine.[16]

---

[16] Christian teaching speaks of God as of personality, but today it is so deformed and void of any meaning that it tells us nothing. The Christian teaching of God actually negates God as personalities in a man, and puts it in theological Holy Trinity, they say God is not an eternal monad, self-sufficient and transcendent One of Neo-Platonism, but *koinonia* or the union of the Three Personalities, eternal and equal. However that is, once again, an imaginary and abstract theological performance debated over for centuries for the sole purpose of not seeing the obvious and that is the story or the event of God who embodies as a person. into his son, and is actually pointing towards the fact that God as a person embodies every man with the human soul who becomes the complete personality, that every complete personality cannot be anything but the living personification of God. Every incomplete personality is merely an individual man, split by the multitude of I. Every complete person is the personification of God. That is what makes it complete. It is not only Christ. He is only the role model and the teacher of this completeness because he actually said: "You are all the sons of God" (John 10.34; Matthew 5:45; John 1.12, to the Romans 8.14, to the Galatians 3.26)

The expression personality I use in a somewhat different meaning here than usual. It is common for that expression to be used derived from the Greek notion *persona*, which represents a mask someone puts in front of the face in order to act a role of some kind. With this act he presents the false I. In this specific instant, I associate persona with personification, so the personality here is the personification of something higher, when man becomes the personification of spirit and when he has one true I in himself, when he is aware of himself in the absolute sense, then it is a personification of this authentic consciousness of himself and displays his true, complete personality, his true face, not the mask or the *persona*. In the following text it will be clear that one can become such a person by working on himself and the transcendental

This is why the organic world exists for the soul to enter the physical body and start the drama of life. The organic life is self-sufficient for the survival of the species. Higher dimension of life happens with the drama of life that human souls experience in the bodies. All plots, comedies and tragedies that existence can offer a human body in all the situations always demand and force the understanding of the meaning of the existence. This *effort towards the understanding of the meaning creates the personality of man*. It lifts the man above the causality of the natural survival. This is how the consciousness is introduced to the organic life: through the understanding of the drama of life in the personality of man, his cognition of the meaning of life which can be acquired only after abundant life experience. The personality of man in the organic world is like a small replica of the Divine in comparison to the existence itself.

Consciousness in the organic world gathers impressions on four levels of events:

1   Through the combinations of the elements themselves, spontaneously or under external influences; this is the world of minerals.

2   Through the symbiosis of elements in a living form and movement which is limited to adjusting organisms to the environment and survival by the very shaping; this is the world of plants.

3   Through the free movement and forming organisms in space and coping with the survival; this is the world of animals.

4   Through the free movement which surpasses the issue of the survival itself and tries out all others contents, every possible deed and misdeed, the drama of life that consolidates all other experiences, that do not merely concern the body, but the mind and the feelings as well. This is the world of people.

---

experiences which the phony split personality cannot have. When we speak of "the person", we always have in mind a complete personality, and when we speak of "I", we always speak of the split I.

While the organic reproduction is the peak of the animal-like existence, that is perception of the Divine, the peak of human existence goes beyond the simple reproduction, man experiences the drama of all the possible experiences, his own and others', events and relationships, and ascends to the meaning of the overall existence. For this purpose, of all the beings that exist only man uses imagination. It is needed for the enrichment of the contents of drama of life experiences. Imagination is the presence of the higher dimensions (air, fire, water) in the lowest, physical reality (earth). Imagination is the ability of compressing the time and space (the characteristic of higher dimensions) for the purpose of designing the meaning of events of all the possibilities of existence in time and space. In imagination we recapitulate the past and imagine the future in order to shape and change the present creatively.

In what way has the presence of imagination been developing in the physical life of man? Since time immemorial imagination has had a leading role in human existence.[17] For centuries by the fireplace imagination was cultivated by telling stories of the ancestors and gods, condensed into archetypes and fairy tales. The forming of the theater scene turned the story into living experience and a plastic event, both personal and collective. In antique dramas all the events of human and divine existence alike were designed in an organized and creative way – in order to be returned to the Divine. Therefore, the performing of drama in archaic times was a sacred, religious act. In those days imagination was one and the same with life. Nowadays it has been degraded to simulacra and simulation.[18] The most general use of imagination happens in the arrangement of the living space. Architecture is the roughest materialization of imagination, but also the most practical. Afterwards, the development of technology presents an even finer and more versatile use of imagination in experiencing the world and all the possibilities of existence[19]. Letter and literature are even finer uses of imagination, and together with them all the experience of the existence has been

---

[17] Elemir Zola: "Uses of Imagination and the Decline of the West".

[18] Jean Baudrillard: "Simulacra and Simulation".

[19] Heidegger: "The Question Concerning Technology", "The End of Philosophy and the Task of Thinking".

collected, and the artistic expression, painting and poetry, are the finest. Science was invented as a need for transforming the imagination into something concrete and practical. Science is also the imaginative compression of space and time, but only for the purpose of designing natural laws; in it we design what was, and what based on the accumulated experience could be, in order to be able to change and create what is now, more accurately what is. Religious imagination designs spiritual laws with the intent to bring man close to the sense. In this it is successful only to the point it finally discovers that man is the sense itself. Therefore we have three types of imagination: the scientific one that designs the natural laws, the artistic one that designs all the experiences of human existence and the religious one that epitomizes all the spiritual experiences into the meaning of the overall existence and consequently ties it to the Divine.

All of this, all the nature and its transformation through technology and culture, unfolds in the presence of incarnated souls. Souls are the virtual centres or magnets which by their mere presence attract all these happenings around themselves. When the soul incarnates into the body, from the higher dimensions to the lower, it as a magnet induces the process of transformation of nature around itself, information as thoughts (air), energy (fire), virtual shapes (water) and physical shapes (earth). That is how all the architecture, technology, science, art and religion come about, everything that is constructive and destructive – because all the options need to be experienced – as processes thanks to which designing and the perception of nature take place, respectively all the powers of existence, and as such are returned to the Divine through the knowing of their meaning. Perception of the Divine is neither one-sided nor passive. It is a two-way thing and pretty active. It simultaneously changes and creates objects of perception.

Souls don't do anything, they are merely the silent witnesses of existence. Nature is the one that does everything in connection with the soul attracted by its Divine splendor. Starting with thoughts – they are the finest vibrations of nature, with which the nature designs itself through the being of man in which the soul resides, whatever a man looks at he designs it, and having done so he returns the meaning to the Divine through his soul – through the action organs of the man's body by means of which he cultivates the nature. Nature does it all in order to enable the perception to the souls. That is the ultimate goal of the organic world.

More precisely, not even the nature does anything, it is unconscious and inert. Work takes place because of the mutual presence of nature and souls, their proximity, like the magnetic induction, when two magnets move one another due to their mere presence. That is why this proximity enables the appearance of the very organic world and life.

The proximity and the contact of soul and the nature happen only in the man's being. Therefore, he is the only creative being. Due to the proximity and the contact of the Divine soul and the manifested world of nature in the man's being, the creative work of man takes place, and work is the essence of the man's existence in this world. *Man's work is the complete realization of the perception of the Divine in this world. Man through his work shapes and returns the acquired perception of existence back to the Divine*. It is the essence of *karma*. That is why in the best writing about *karma, Bhagavad Gita*, the essence of *karma* was described as the work that is God's, not man's. Man best realizes his *karma* when he does everything as though God worked through him, and does not ask for any rewards or results of the work for himself, but only works as the extended hand of God. The same idea is expressed by the Gnostics when they claim that the man's soul is an extended hand of the Divine creation.

10. PERSONALITY AS THE PERSONIFICATION OF THE DIVINE

With the appearance of the human body the organic life transfers to a higher plain, it is no longer just an issue of reproduction for the sake of the survival, it becomes a stage for the drama of life, for trying out all possibilities for action of the higher order, all possible events, not just a simple shaping of organic and inorganic being. Events are advanced by means of tools and instruments, by action which involves thinking, feeling and the will of an individual and its interaction, the development of the civilization, technology and culture. Only an interaction of this sort can crystallize the personality in man. Only a complete personality in man the Divine personality can reflect because the Divine is always manifested as a personality. Only when it is itself, the impersonal Absolute remains. The basic aspiration of the Divine is to become concrete. More than anything else it wishes to know itself even in the most inferior role. It always aspires to manifest itself as a personality through which it becomes concrete and active, conceived and clear in all the possible aspects and experiences, subjective and objective alike. *The act of manifesting the world is a reflection of the aspiration of the Divine to manifest itself as a personality. In the complete personality of man, as the personification of the Divine finalizes and conceives all the manifestation of the world.*

From the very nature of the organic world it is clear that it can provide nothing for itself but the conditions for the organic reproduction and survival. It is its peak. As well as the development of the inorganic world organic is based on spontaneous mechanical laws of causality, and an occasional coincidence. For the transformation and action of the higher order, for the meaningful work and culture, an impulse from high above is needed, from the Divine consciousness. It arrives in the organic world in the form of human souls.

A complete personality means wholeness in the sense of existence, unity, and a complete person is always the same, although it is familiar with assorted experiences.

Therefore a complete person comes only at the end of the process of individuation, maturing through all the experiences of perception and action in the drama of life.

Up until that moment, the personality is split up into the multitude of I's and subjugated by the versatility of impressions it keeps collecting along the way.

Before maturing enough to form the human body, all inherited experiences of being have shaped certain impressions or characteristics.[20] They act as the little personalities, as individual I, like all the entities that form spontaneously. Therefore in the human form they continue to behave like a multitude of small personalities or the multitude of I's. When a human soul is incarnated into a human body, as the complete personification of the Divine, it faces the action of the multitude of I's in that being. The entire human life and all the maturing of people boils down to comprehending, designing, consolidating, and overcoming all those special characteristics of I's into one whole person, one consciousness and one will. When this happens it is called enlightenment or self-knowledge. The word means getting to know oneself, recognizing the soul for what it is independent of the body, during the time it resides in the body. This shows that while the soul is dwelling in the body it is tainted by the multitude of I's from the experiences of inferior shapes of particular being. Its self-knowing means that those experiences have been designed and made aware of in a higher context and understanding, as the aspects of the existence of nature as such, and surpassed, but all in the context of the Divine that enables it all.

The multitude of I's has a creative function, it facilitates the exchange of experiences among various kinds of impressions, doubts and insights into the opposite, and the consciousness of opposites enables the consciousness of the choice.

If, on the other hand, many I's, for some reason, are incapable of knowing using this creative way, the multitude of I's is a cause of confusion and illusion.

---

[20] In "Yoga Sutras" Patanjali calls them *vasana* and *samskara*, deeper and shallow impressions, that have been unconsciously gathered over many reincarnations. In modern psychology they are referred to as contents of the unconscious.

The holographic nature of reality makes all the confusion and conflicts reflect the world around us, and the events that (seemingly or really) happen to us. All conflicts between people are a direct consequence of the division that exists inside of people.

Consolidating all the impressions of particular experiences, of all I's, the attaining of peace and the perfection of the whole person as the personification of the Divine, is possible only through love. *Love is the strength that consolidates the differences with its complete understanding of the matter. Without love understanding is not possible. Love as the factor which consolidates everything comes from the nature of the universal Field or the Divine matrix, whose primary characteristic is unity outside of the numerous differences.* Love is the only real expression of the true knowing of the meaning of life, the only real expression of the complete personality. This explains why God is love, and only the ability of giving unconditional love returns man to the Divine.

11. DIVINE AS THE FOUNDATION
OF THE SOUL

What would be the definition of soul?

It is a fragment of the broken up holograph of the Divine Absolute that contains and reflects the entire Absolute.

This fragment manifests itself as the pure energy in higher dimensions.

Since the word *energeia* means "being in movement, manifesting itself, and acting",[21] the original expression of the Divine movement and action manifests itself as the uncreated light.

As this uncreated light goes down to the lower dimensions, it becomes Word or Logos in the element of Air, will or intention in the element of Fire, and in the element of Water or the astral world it shows itself as the created light stronger than the sun, and the feeling of pure bliss.

In the element of Earth, the physical realm, the Divine presence manifests itself as the light of the stars, as the life energy, as beauty and harmony, and as the act of good will, love and compassion. Those are all concrete, material manifestations of Divine presence.

This is the light that the dying see as their soul or the souls of other people.[22] It is followed by the feeling of immense bliss. Because of the illusory identification with the body, the dying see their dying soul as if it were on the outside coming in the shape of the light. When a man overcomes every illusion of individuality and identification with the body and mind, he will recognize this

---

[21] The Greek original under energy understands every movement in existence, in being, the movement alone is energy. Since everything moves, then everything can be seen as energy. But today our tongue has darkened the view of existence as energy, we see everything as "dead matter" and under energy, we understand only what we produce by combustion or electricity. Only quantum physics and mysticism today remind us that matter does not exist, but everything is just energy.

[22] In the books that deal with this sort of matter, frequently this light is mistaken for the Guardian Angel or it is given religious names (most commonly Jesus).

light as himself, or more accurately, God will be The One Who Is in this personality, and the illusion of man will disappear.

Nature being a reflection of the absolute consciousness was not created in time, rather time is merely a shape of the relative event within the nature, it is pointless to contemplate on the beginning of nature's creation. That is why in nature a seemingly paradoxical event is possible, that consequence precedes the cause, or more popularly known as the "laws of attraction", that we can make something happen if in the world of ideas or imagination we perceive that it has already happened. This is what attracts it.

Since it is timeless, the Divine is omnipresent, independent, and present as a condition and foundation for existence itself. Divine, being timeless, is always conceived and manifested as the present moment in the illusion of time.

On the other hand, the mere fact that nature did not originate in a specific point in time means that the Divine's experience of its own existence it does not receive through the projection of its souls over the course of time – it is already in it. Since space is connected with time, it means that none of the experiences of the existence are separated from the Divine. Only the Divine exists and that is the only reality.

The whole drama of awakening discussed here is merely the awakening of the One who is in its most individual aspect, as an individual soul. When the Absolute is The Wholeness, it does not need any awakening because it cannot be unconscious. It individualizes itself into various proportions of manifestation leading to the individual soul and with this individualization it falls deeper and deeper into oblivion keeping itself occupied with events of various kinds. The final goal is for the Wholeness to be aware of itself in the most individualized form, as a man, after all those experiences. This is the way how the Whole really becomes complete. If it could particularize and project itself without losing its consciousness and wholeness, it would not be perfect or complete. Its self-knowledge in the individual soul, after all the suffering and the illusion of separation, is a proof and the manifestation of its wholeness and perfection.

Nothing is outside the Absolute. Since our souls are never separated from the Divine from which they originate, all of it is happening in the man, as our awakening.

Therefore, besides the present moment, Divine is always here, present.

Meaning: always here and now. Never in time or separated from anything.

For this reason reality is made up of paradoxes that there is the outside world with all these events of nature, like they are all happening in us. On the outside only the present is taking place, and the consciousness of the past and the future exists in us. Those are two parallel realities that have a common source. Those two parallel realities manifest as the inner and the outer, as the consciousness and unconsciousness, as subjective and objective.

Differences only appear when viewed from a different focal point.

If we observe from the pure awareness of ourselves nothing has been created, there is nothing objective, only the Divine Absolute exists as the existence itself of here and now.

If we observe from the perspective of an individual being, as the fragment of the holograph, there is the inner and the outer, and the whole story of the creation of the objective world seems plausible.

In order to satisfy the illusion of existence, for otherwise we would not be writing all of this, we shall say that the souls are timeless presence of the Divine consciousness in the illusion of time.

The Divine does not project itself in the form of the individual souls, as it is popularly imagined when the mind is identified with the body, it cannot project itself because nothing is possible outside of itself. Divine itself exists only as the existence, as the consciousness itself. The illusion of individuality of that consciousness is what is called the individual souls, and the bigger the illusion, the more it seems that those souls are individual, that they get reincarnated and mature gradually. That is why when the human soul wakes up from its illusion, it sees that it does not exist, only the Divine exists.

On the other hand, the Divine itself is not in the illusion. Everything else that exists in any way, shape or form does so outside the Divine.

Everything being inside of the Divine, and the Divine being the reality itself, it means that everything is reality, even that what we call the illusion here. Generally, illusion is something that does not exist in reality. Hence, the states of illusory being exist, such as individual souls that are born and change over the course of time, and suffer *karma*, are states that are real, although illusory. Illusion of existence exists in reality, even though it is still an illusion.

This gives dual nature to the existence: on the one hand, it is tested as an illusion and a state of suffering, and on the other hand, it is always possible to overcome this state, because it is illusory. Only by perceiving reality for what it is relieves us of the illusion and the suffering.

To avoid diluting this matter further, as the dialectics of emptiness (*sunyata*), something that Nagarjuna did already, we shall return to the heart of the matter, to explaining what souls are in a way that we can do something practically with this definition.

12. THE PRESENCE OF THE DIVINE AS A TESTIMONY

A soul is the presence of the Divine in the existence itself.

A silent presence, the testimony itself.

All of the creation and manifestation of the universe, however illusory it may seem, did not happen outside of the Divine, because nothing can be outside of it, for it is the Absolute. Thus, the Divine is always present in everything created and manifested, in every shape, in every being and in every event.

The presence of the Divine inspires the nature to shape, perfect and conform itself to the Divine.

This conformance of nature is the overall cosmos and all the life that exists.

The final perfection of the nature`s shaping toward the Divine is a human being.

The final perfection of the reflecting of the Divine in nature is a Man's self-consciousness, Self, and self-knowledge.

The Divine is present beyond the time of the happening of the shapes, beings and events, as transcendental basis, the one that facilitates everything. It is present here and now. If it were not so, if the Divine were not beyond time, if it were not transcendental, there would be no difference between the Divine and the manifested world. That is, there would be no manifested world just the Divine.

The presence of the Divine in everything as a testimony is always outside of all events, never in them. It is outside of everything, transcendental. That is why it is called testimony: the witness is not a participant in the event but merely an observer. Thanks to the witness the events become public, known and conscious. Without the witness it would go blindly following the laws of causality and it would never reach any purpose or meaning. It would be no different from the invisible work of the bacteria. Likewise, if the witness were not outside of the happening, if it were one with it, it could not be objectively conscious of itself or the world. For the objective consciousness it takes differentiation, distinction. *If the Divine were not transcendental, there would be no consciousness in nature, or the awareness of existence as such. There would be no man as the carrier of such a consciousness.* But then again, if the Divine were not immanent to existence, the existence would not exist, because nothing exists of its own accord, then the nature itself that is unconscious can ever become conscious. The transcendental nature of the Divine is discussed only because of the limitations of the Man's mind, never because of the Divine itself, because it is not transcendental or immanent. It itself is, as an Absolute.

The Divine testimony is not like the common human testimony of something. *The presence of the Divine testimony is the strongest driving force that there is: being the Absolute, it as the immanent gives incentive for manifestation, and transcendental attracts all the emanation toward the purpose or sense. Everything takes place because of this presence, because the whole universe is manifested as such to act as a reflection of the Divine consciousness of itself. The presence of the Divine as a witness is the biggest attractor of all the happening. It is a magnet that shapes every event of nature. The whole nature exists because of it, and not for itself.*

The subtle, timeless presence of the Divine in every form of existence is the consciousness and intention we see in every life form, in every living cell, in every event, that gives warmth, life and the meaning to it all. The presence of the Divine through human soul is the cause of the start of the civilization, culture and technology through man and Man's actions, that, by far, surpass the simple organic and inorganic shaping.

The very presence of the souls in nature transforms and trans substantializes the entire nature towards a higher sense, towards its personalization of the Divine, in order to become the perfect mirror of the Divine consciousness of itself.

Although, it transforms itself on the outside it becomes the perfect mirror of the Divine awareness of itself only in the complete personality of man as the personification of the Divine. All of the outer transformation, material and spiritual culture, is merely a shadow of the process of individuation and becoming whole, and Man's embodiment in the Divine personality as the living presence of the Divine.

Although the Divine is already present as the presence itself, it becomes the living and efficient presence as love in the complete personality of man.

13. THE MECHANICAL MANIFESTATION OF THE ORGANIC WORLD

The manifestation of the universe has its mechanical aspect, as well. For the greatest part it has developed spontaneously according to the mechanical, and mathematical laws of causal development and multiplication (The Law of Number Three, The Law of Number Seven, etc.). Practically, all inorganic world came into being in accordance with those mechanical laws, spontaneously, without the participation of the consciousness. Most of the cosmos is comprised of this inorganic world.

All higher dimensions, lower and higher astral, are a part of inorganic, mechanical and unconscious emanation and shaping.

We have already stated that every action creates patterns or fields that have a feedback effect on the further action, on shaping someone similar to oneself. This is the way inorganic entities originated spontaneously shaping themselves in higher dimensions, mostly astral, because astral is the closest to the material plain of concrete shapes and creations, that is the reason why it is the easiest to create and keep a specific shape in astral.

These inorganic entities are natural elementals, spirits and demons. They originated spontaneously together with the unconscious multiplying of the inorganic world in all the dimensions.

Their primary characteristic is a heartless fight for their survival. They do not possess the higher functions of personality due to the lack of soul and the meaning of existence. The only one who possesses that is the man in the organic world. The inorganic plain does not create its own energy. Energy is being created and accumulated only by the organic beings in the three-dimensional physical world. Accumulation and preservation are, besides inertia, one of the characteristics of the physical world. This is why the inorganic beings have to take energy from the organic ones like parasites. Since they live on higher dimensions than that of the physical plain, they manipulate beings in the physical world, who are limited by their physical senses and cannot clearly distinguish the influences of the higher plains, they possess the three-dimensional beings and force them to act in such a manner that they provide food for their parasites. However, since they are natural dwellers of the higher plains, especially astral, their food is not physical food, but energetic, made up of special frequencies created by the beings that radiate them, emotions of especially low frequency, such as negative emotions, hatred, fear and suffering. Inorganic beings drive all organic beings into the type of behavior that induces the emotions of hatred, fear and suffering – and they especially force a man to behave in this negative way.

14. THE MANIFESTATION OF THE ORGANIC WORLD AS THE BASIS FOR CONSCIOUSNESS

The purpose of the entire manifestation of the universe is to act as the foundation for mirroring the Divine consciousness of itself. For this mirroring only inorganic, spontaneous and mechanical manifestation was not enough. The organic world was necessary in which the action of a higher order would develop from the spontaneous causation and coincidence which exists in the inorganic area. This action is what brings drama into existence and life, contents and meaning, the evolution of all the possible experiences so that the consciousness of the Divine of itself could be complete as a personality.

This life drama, work and fight for the purpose, is what is called *karma* in the Indian tradition.

Karma is only possible in the organic world, the three-dimensional physical world that exists on planet Earth. And the way it exists only in the man. Lower life forms do not possess *karma*. They only have existence and living.

In the creation of the organic world all higher dimensions participate, the purpose of their existence is to create the organic three-dimensional life. The causality of *karma* extends to the higher dimensions for this very reason. We do not see the whole causation chain for our senses and the physical mind sees only what is physical in our immediate surroundings. That is why we can see only the consequences and parts of causality that have brought about some consequences.

Only in the completely developed organic world and life there are conditions for the complete reflection of the Divine consciousness of itself.

The Divine consciousness always reflects itself as the personality, that is the personal, entirely its own, distinctive. Divine is always a personality, and that is why it can reflect itself and become aware of only in a complete personality.

The creation of those conditions had its evolution, they did not originate all at once. It is the evolution of all the living forms up until the creation of the human body at the end of the evolution. Only human body has all the sense organs for perception and the action organs. That is why only the human body is suitable for the presence of the complete Divine consciousness.

Only the human body is capable of the Divine presence which we call a soul.

The Divine is present in all the other forms of organic life, in plants and animals, but to a far lesser degree, as much as it is necessary for the basic life and survival and the gathering of the kind of experiences without creating *karma* and life drama of a personality.

The purpose of the overall evolution of the organic life is in the creation of the conditions for the forming of the personality. The personality is formed through the drama of life. For this drama a fully formed organic life is needed, in effect, far above the simple reproduction and the struggle for survival.

The merging of the Divine presence as the soul with the human body will be easier to comprehend if we picture a soul as a man and the body as the mirror in which the man is watching in order to see himself objectively. For the soul that originates from the Divine, to be able to manifest and affirm fully all the way to the physical realm, it takes a corresponding form in nature, as accurate as the image in the mirror. This accurate image the nature shaped into the human body to be a suitable form for the presence of the human soul, the emanation of the Divine. That is why we speak of the body as of the physical aspect of the soul, its manifested and effective aspect, while the soul itself is transcendental and unexpressed. As well as the Divine whose personification it represents. The body where the soul resides has both its astral and the energetic aspects that surpass the physical body, it contains the ethereal, astral and the mental body. The soul functions with them on higher dimensions. That is why the body consists of all the dimensions. That is why those higher dimensions are in man, not outside of him.

Man is a combination of two factors: transcendental soul, or the Divine presence, and the body as an individuation process of nature. For this reason man has a dual nature, he is capable of reaching the Divine heavens and the bottom of hell. Man can be animal but also Divine. His self-realization is reflected in the uplifting above the natural conditioning, away from everything that is physical, mechanical, conditioning. Everything that possesses consciousness, goodness, independence and objectivity got this from the Divine presence that constitutes his soul. Everything that causes suffering and ignorance comes from the identification with the body.

Man is a bridge between everything naturally manifested and the Divine.

The Divine is most strongly present in the existence manifesting through the man's soul.

15. THE CIRCLE OF CREATION: INORGANIC WORLD, ORGANIC WORLD AND MAN

If the whole process of the Divine self-knowledge or existence can be imagined as a sphere, which would be in accordance with the ancient tradition, depicting a circle for simplicity, the beginning of the circle would be a spontaneous manifestation of the inorganic world through the seven phases and the five dimensions, through the fall into the lower and rougher states. Reaching the outermost opposite point from the start of the circle would be the origin of the organic world, as the beginning of the turning and the return to source. Man with the soul would be the ascending line of the other half of the circle that finalizes the whole, the return to the Divine origin.

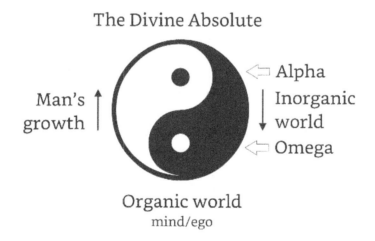

The Divine Absolute

Man's growth

Alpha
Inorganic world
Omega

Organic world
mind/ego

Based on this chart we shall explain the further details of the emanation of the Divine.

Firstly, we can see the circle as the Divine Wholeness, which shows that everything happens in it as itself; then circling as a way of emanating The Wholeness; then moving along the descending line through the inorganic world, reaching the outermost lowest point of the organic world, and the beginning of the ascending line through the man's growth and going back to the outcome in the Divine Absolute.

The first part of the manifestation follows the ascending line through the inorganic world and all the proportions. It is the mechanical complexity of nature with the growing number of conditioning laws, through the intercrossing of the frequencies in higher dimensions, and atoms and molecules in the physical plain.

When it reaches the end of its spontaneous, mechanical manifestation in accordance with the law of number seven, the forming of the organic world happens, on the opposite end of the circle of the manifestation of the Divine Absolute. The organic world is the peak of the mechanical and unconscious manifestation and the beginning of creating the conditions for the conscious work through the shaping of all the sense and action organs and the man's body. The organic world becomes a mirror for reflecting the Divine consciousness.

In the organic world the action of a higher order begins, while in the inorganic sphere there was just a mechanical movement of the subatomic, atomic, and the chemical processes, in the organic area forms the movement of the higher order, and those are more complex activities and events of the organic combinations that have originated in subatomic, atomic and chemical processes, events and happenings of the more complex wholes, physical bodies.

The events in the organic world vary from coping with the survival to the dramatic events in search for the meaning of survival, amongst beings who have all organic abilities of sensory perception and action among the people.

The drama of life forms the personality of man.

Soul as the personification of the Divine consciousness incarnates only in the human shape.

The soul keeps incarnating in human form until it experiences all the aspects of the purpose of all the happenings in life.

Before that the consciousness of the Divine is indirectly present in the plant and animal life on the level of species, as elementary condition to serve the purpose of being the carrier of life, and to be experienced and active in all the forms.

The soul was not incarnated in them in its entirety, but only a fraction of the soul, only to the degree it takes for it to gather all the impressions. The soul was merely practicing in them the ability of staying in the three-dimensional world in an elementary way, with the possibility of simple movements and survival on land, water and air.

The collection of all the impressions of movement and survival in the physical world, which the Divine consciousness collects through experiences of existence of the plant and the animal world, enables incarnation in the human body and the start of growth towards the meaning of existence.

The soul does not incarnate in its entirety, whole, in the human body either, but only a part of it, still a bigger part than in animals. In the human body it reincarnates as much as it takes for it to gather impressions connected to that reincarnation. The soul never incarnates whole, it is impossible because of its Divine grandeur.

It is important to know that soul simultaneously divides in its projections and incarnations because of its Divine grandeur. This is the reason why we have a feeling of closeness with all the animals, and all the living beings. Since it is outside time and space the soul also splits itself in terms of time and space, more precisely, it can simultaneously exist in several places, and in more bodies, and at the same time in different epochs. This is a way of a rapid gathering of experiences. This is what it always does. Only from the perspective of a mind limited by the body, time and space, it seems like the soul incarnates during linear time and moves from life to life. It lives all of its lives at the same time, because for the soul there is no time. All human souls, seemingly divided by the bodies in space, in individual experiences, in its final outcome are one. Soul is one like the Divine that personifies it is one. However, it is only in the highest proportion, here where we are it seems divided into multitude. Therefore, we must speak of it in accordance with the proportion we are in.

The experience of life of a soul in the organic form and in the human body, is completely conditioned the same as the organic world, and those are influences of a wider scope from the higher dimensions, namely the impact of the planets. This impact is thoroughly shown by the science of Astrology.

When the experience of existence matures enough in the human form, it starts to follow a rising path. Then the overcoming of the conditionality starts, the overcoming that creates the human body, and the sensory world in general. Man meets higher worlds, higher knowledge, and strives towards liberation. Man's existence becomes positive at the point where he starts to overcome the identification with the body and mind, when he starts to rise. At that point the nature gives him support in all possible ways because its primary function is to serve to liberate the man's spirit. For as long as he falls for the trap of identifying with the body and mind the man experiences suffering and a conflict with nature.

The final liberation is the return to God's outcome.

The entire circling happens within the Divine outcome as his imagination or a dream.

Therefore, only the awakening is the outcome of all the happening, and not achieving of anything new.

Awakening happens only in the human form, in a man who has become the individual personification of the Divine.

The Absolute itself doesn't need any awakening. The confirmation or actualization of its absolute perfection happens through a man, when from the unconscious state of an individual alienated from the Divine wholeness and the suffering in all the illusions that alienation brings, with the work on himself and his will, he recognizes the whole process of falling into the illusion and the necessity of awakening, and returning to the Wholeness through the consciousness of Himself, his own essence, the Divine Absolute itself, for nothing outside of it is possible. That process happens in a man as the awakening, and that is the only "salvation of the soul" which can take place.

Practically, all a man needs is awakening.

In that awakening a man disappears and only the Divine Wholeness remains.

That would be the schematic view of the whole process.

We shall deal now with the details of the life dramas a soul experiences in human incarnations. But before we take a look at the incarnations of the souls in this world, in bodies we have now, we must understand their existence before this world.

16. ON THE INCARNATIONS OF SOULS BEFORE THE ORGANIC LIFE ON EARTH

In higher dimensions the crisscrossing of frequencies and proportions creates inorganic beings whose way of life is a constant struggle for survival.

Inorganic beings come into existence based on the fact that the consciousness of the Divine always manifests in two ways: as a form of all the happenings and as personality. Personality gives sense to the forming of the events. The soul as personality manifests only in the human form.

The other name for what we call here a Divine manifestation as a personality in its original state is monad. Souls originally exist as the Divine monads which design the shaping on both the inorganic and the organic plain.

Souls, as the principles of consciousness, never manifest themselves in their entirety or to a sufficient degree for a being to become a conscious personality in either organic or the inorganic world. Only in the human body the soul as a principle of consciousness manifests enough to be able to be shaped as a person. However, the souls do not manifest themselves fully there either, its presence in a man grows proportionally to the man's growth, the man's becoming a complete personality, that is the personification of the Divine. The more complete the man is the more the entire soul manifests through him. The more divided and unconscious, the less the Divine consciousness of soul is present in him.

In all the inorganic and organic living beings the principle of consciousness is present only to a small degree, less than needed for the forming of the personality, just about enough for the basic survival and the gathering of impressions.

In the inorganic area, the shaping of the conscious entities as inorganic beings, goes one way only: towards the survival never towards the essence. Similar to the animals in the organic world, inorganic beings are not so conscious of themselves as the subjects of the happening but are more likely to be directed towards the objects, reacting to the outer stimuli and the survival itself. It corresponds to the nature of the inorganic world, it is still on the level of just manifesting and shaping – and creating the conditions for the appearance of the organic life.

Only in the organic life the Divine consciousness reflects itself completely so that we call this reflecting a soul.

The organic world is the mirror in which the Divine reflects. Inorganic world does not have these qualities as of yet, it is still very much an incomplete world, the world of elements and elementals. Therefore, the Divine consciousness cannot reflect itself in it. It can only act and manifest itself in all sorts of ways, and is, for this reason, the area of the growing conditionality, and it falls down to the lower spheres.

Only when all the conditions are met in the organic world for the complete sensory perception, designing and the creative personal deeds, the Divine consciousness can completely reflect itself.

Reflection of the Divine consciousness in the organic world is what we call a soul and the incarnation of a soul in a body. Only in this case the Divine reflects itself, everything else is impersonal existence.

It does not happen from the first take. Sometimes it is necessary to make several attempts to make it right, improving, gathering experiences in all the drama of life that the organic world provides. This gathering of experiences and aiming for perfection is the act of polishing the mirror so that the soul, the Divine consciousness, can clearly and accurately reflect itself. That mirror polishing are the incarnations and rebirthing of souls, as well as the meaning of the life dramas.

The drama of life can be known by the personality individually, or more precisely, it can be known only personally, through the process of individuation. Since the organic world is always in the three-dimensional space and time, the acquiring of experiences does not happen concurrently but always individually. Therefore, the collective "salvation of souls", the collective "resurrection" of all people one fine "judgement day" is an impossibility. Every story promising the collective salvation of people was concocted with the purpose of deceiving people regarding the true nature of their lives and development. The salvation is always a process of individuation that extends onto several incarnations.

It is imperative to stress here a simple fact that people generally overlook: the polishing of the mirror is just that. Nothing else. Only polishing gives clarity, the mirror can in no other way be made but by polishing, smoothing uneven surfaces, removing blemishes and stains. Removal of everything that soils the purity of the open presence of the Divine. This purity is the consciousness of the Divine.

It is a path of purification.[23] It is the foundation of all the ethics and all morality. The essence of all the knowledge.

The clarity of such purification enables God to reflect himself for what he really is. This time, however, not only as an abstract Absolute, but as a specific individual, a man. God reflects in the man's Self, the most intimate meeting point of all the experiences of life.

The clarity of such reflection turns the scheme of events upwards, towards the outcome, the Divine goes back to itself by the knowing of itself in its most intimate expression, the man's heart.

In the chart it is marked as the rising part of the circle and man's development.

The Divine consciousness, which reflects itself incompletely in everything, gives with this act life to the inorganic beings, as well. They, due to their lacking in completeness, have no real reflection of the soul or the Divine consciousness. They have as much consciousness as it takes them to survive. Many of them are humble and simple in their lives, but there are many of those beings we can call "heartless" and cruel. They are predators and conquerors. Some of them are as old as the universe.

Same as with the incarnations of souls, it is not enough to have just one incarnation for acquiring the necessary impressions and the experiences of the consciousness, it takes more, in the same way the forming of organic life on one place in cosmos was not enough. More experiments were required.

Due to the overall balance and development along the lines of the dialectics of opposites, the divine consciousness has created both: the positive and the negative entities of its own consciousness. *In the divine wholeness the negative entities (the Satanic*

---

[23] This is how Buddha called his teaching. The purification of a being for the presence of a higher consciousness is exactly what Buddhism is.

and Luciferian forces) take up one third, and the positive entities (angelic and human) take up two thirds. It takes double the power of good to overthrow evil.

As a result of this fact, astral on Earth is contaminated with inorganic entities and demons who affect human lives, that it is safe to say that no man is spared their influence. Actually, the few people who are above their influence, are called saints. Their aura radiates with its beneficial purity all round. Those are highly developed souls.

In connection with this it is important to know one more fact about souls: how to distinguish them according to the level of their maturity and age.

17. THE DIVISION OF SOULS: THE YOUNG, DEVELOPED AND HIGHLY DEVELOPED

First of all, it must be said that this division is only ostensible. The souls are a reflection of the Divine consciousness in the human body, and as such cannot be young or old like the physical bodies which are created in time, and as such the souls cannot grow. They are all timeless and one in the Divine consciousness. Time, or the concept of it we know, exists only in the three-dimensional organic world, on the surfaces of the planets.

Still, there is a difference in the incarnated souls regarding their maturity and the type of experiences they are trying out, some seem like young and they need more rudimentary experiences, while others seem old and experienced, they understand quicker and better all the events and their conduct is more mature. Some souls dig deeper in the experiences of life and the temptations, but there are those as well who wish to get rid of the temptations of life, like they have had enough.

The division to young, medium and the highly developed souls is merely the division to the percentage of the soul being present in the body. The young ones are with the smallest percentage in the body, the medium ones have a higher level of presence, and the highly developed souls are the ones with the highest percentage of presence in the body.

Those differences also exist in the number of incarnations. Every soul has its cycle of incarnations it goes through, some souls started them sooner and are currently finishing them, while others are just starting the cycle; some go through them faster and more easily, and some more slowly and harder. Because of the illusion of time in this world it seems that some soul is old because it has gone through so many incarnations, and some other one young because it is merely starting the cycle. They are outside the body, in their authentic state they are all the same, only their expression of maturity in the body and between the reincarnations during the cycle of rebirthing is different. Namely, *the soul does not go to its original Divine state after the death of one body.* During the cycle of incarnations it stays in the sphere of higher astral ("the heavenly world") where it relives the impressions of the previous incarnation, recovering from them and getting ready for the next one. For this reason in hypnotic regressions a memory is brought back to mind that is under the impression of the previous lives and also there is a difference in the maturity of the souls, where some are young, and some are old.[24] Hypnotic regression reaches those experiences only, of the heavenly and the earthly world, because it is based on the mind and its subconscious, not on its transcendence.

In the true uplifting of the soul to its Divine goal, those differences and impressions are non-existent, because the cycle of incarnating the body is finalized. With its ending all the seeming differences disappear.[25]

The cycle of reincarnations can best be comprehended using the following chart:

---

[24] This is the case of the best and the most accurate books on the subject of these memories of life between life: Michael Newton: *Journey of Souls*; and Michael Newton: *Destiny of Souls*. These are the only two books I can recommend because I know them to be true. Even though they are relatively incomplete about the whole matter, the level of information they put forward, they do so correctly and truthfully. The books by Raymond Moody: *"Life after life"* and *"The Light Beyond"* are also true. All the other books I have had the opportunity to read are fabrications that please the illusions of Ego.

[25] Of the ending of the whole cycle of rebirthing teaches the original Buddhism as well as Zen Buddhism, which does not deal with solving the problems of one life merely, which later transfers to another life and lives, but to the whole cycle of experiences of rebirthing. This is why Buddhism is above all other teachings and religions. On the cycles of incarnations according to the Sufi teachings plenty of information can be found in the work "God Speaks" by Meher Baba.

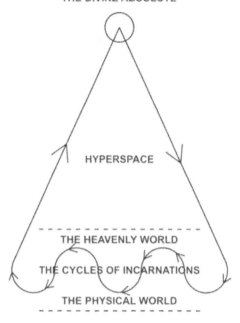

The whole process happens within the Divine because nothing is possible outside of it, and the Divine is the timeless One. Therefore, the whole cycle of the incarnations of souls is only an illusion which appears like that from the three-dimensional plain of the organic world, which is the only place where the experience of the linear time exists, the experience of the individual existence of the persons. From the perspective of the soul all its lives are one life, which is happening at this very moment, like a performance. From our linear perspective we can say that soul simultaneously splits itself into several lives, to all the lives at once, that it does not move in the course of time as an entity. This is what it looks like only from the perspective of the organic world, from the illusion of time. The soul does not waste time going through time, because it has no idea what it is. All its lives are simultaneous, happening at the same time, all the experiences that can be had, only in the mind limited by the body and the Ego it seems to experience everything over a period of time. So, basically, the Judeo- Christian teaching is right when they say there is no reincarnation, but it has been taken out of context in such a way that it hides the whole truth. Reincarnations do exist, but they refer to the experience of mind and Ego, the individual, and not the life of the soul itself, which has one life, eternal, or more precisely timeless. This is why the enlightened say that the soul is neither born nor dies. This is why only the enlightenment is imperative. The awakened see that all the lives are one life, actually they see it as a dream of a soul, and the dream for an enlightened person is something that has not really happened. The whole story of the reincarnations and the understanding of the entire process is necessary for an unconscious mind that is identified with the body, the soul does not need this. Therefore, the story is important because the soul needs to get through to the mind and get to know itself in the body. This getting through to the mind and strengthening the presence in the body is what we see as the degree of maturity of the soul.

The organic world having originated from the inorganic world it is quite understandable that the entities from the inorganic beings will have an effect on the organic beings.

It is all natural in the universe of the free emanation of everything that can be emanated.

Hence, all the temptations of the souls in this world consist not only of the understanding and mastering the organic life, but also to overpower the influences of the inorganic beings, all the dragons, bogeymen, and demons that live there and have no other purpose in life but to be parasites, if not predators and rulers of the organic beings. They, being the way they are, largely contribute to the drama of life and the temptations a man has to overcome in order to become a complete personality.

It is important to know that the influence of the inorganic beings functions following the principle of opposites and polarity. Everything that is manifested contains polarity and the dialectics of opposites. Consequently, inorganic beings function as the opposite of the organic, everything that is good for the organic beings is bad for the inorganic and vice versa. Inorganic beings, not all but some that are particularly negatively oriented, are decidedly opposed to the interest of the people and the human souls, and as a consequence of this they always oppose just for the sake of opposing. In religions they are presented as devils, they are called "the enemy of man" and "adversary". The nature of souls is life and every good deed is the affirmation of life. That is why the nature of all these inorganic beings, especially reptiloid demons from the lower astral, and their hybrids in this world, is only evil and destruction. ***All the lies in this world come from them.***[26] There is the law of trinity at work here, the polarization, that consists of action (1), reaction (2) and solution (3). Action (1) here would be the intention of God to manifest itself as an individual soul in the body, reaction (2) would be the resistance of the inorganic beings, and the consequence or the solution (3) would be a complete personality as the personification of the Divine and the whole presence of a soul in a body. The resistance itself crystallizes the wholeness of a personality.

The whole process of incarnating the souls into body stretches through several incarnations, with the gradual increase of the percentage of the presence of a soul in a body, which manifests as a bigger and a more mature soul.

The span of gradual increase of the presence of soul in the body is what we perceive to be the human civilization and history, and the growth of the human consciousness and culture.

All the evil that exists in this world, all the collective wars and individual crimes, the destruction of nature, all lies and deceit have happened under the influence of the negative inorganic beings on human bodies that do not have enough presence of the consciousness of the soul to be able to make decisions for themselves, and their actions, but are being manipulated and conditioned by the inorganic beings.

Man's soul is incapable of doing evil, its nature is the affirmation of life and all that is good because it is the reflection of the Divine consciousness in this world.

Soul has to experience all the options of existence, all the contradictions. That is why an alien and an opposing force is needed in order to provide a negative experience for the soul, because the souls would never be able to do that themselves.

Therefore, the destructive inorganic beings provide the kind of experiences that the souls could not obtain or experience of their own free will.

---

[26] Jesus said to them: "Ye are of your father the devil, and the lusts of your father ye will do: he was a murderer from the beginning, and abode not in the truth, because there is no truth in him. When he speaketh a lie, he speaketh of his own: for he is a liar, and the father of it." (John, 8, 44.)

The negative inorganic beings have a destructive effect on the world and the people and through people, possessing them and controlling their consciousness. So it appears as though people were doing some evil. Afterwards, through elaborate methods of mind control they convince this person that he or she committed this evil act. It is easier for them to work this way because they use the same body and the same mind. The biggest part of manipulation with the people's consciousness is forcing people to identify with the body and mind, and rigging the objective consciousness of the wider context. This way people begin to develop the feeling of guilt and the mentality of the sinner which as the final outcome has committing more crimes. The problem is that not all people are mature enough to resist it, most souls on this planet have very little experience of living in the human bodies. That is why they fall prey to the more experienced, older entities.

Only the body used by the young and inexperienced souls can be possessed by the astral entities. The soul itself cannot be possessed or put in jeopardy in any way. Only the body can be possessed, especially the body over which the soul does not have command. All the maturing of souls in this world has a purpose, amongst everything else, to reclaim its dominion and its will in the physical body.

On this planet approximately 90 per cent of people are young souls.

That is the reason why this world is the way it is.

The remaining ten per cent are older and more advanced souls that get incarnated here for the reason of developing tolerance towards the young souls, as well as the skills in teaching them. It is imperative to set oneself free. In order for this freeing to get the objective value, the freed one must help the others to set themselves free.

Therefore, the number of people who are not possessed, who are not under the influence of the inorganic beings, is minuscule.

Actually, the biggest part of the process of the liberation of souls in this world is to learn to recognize the impact of the inorganic influences and to learn to set themselves free from them. So-called enlightenment, the resurrection, or setting your soul free is nothing but the increase of the percentage of the presence of the soul in the body to such an extent that it has become so dominant over all the other influences, both the organic, and the inorganic.

Since a large part of the inorganic world extends to the higher dimensions, or astral, those higher dimensions being the inner dimensions of man, his unconscious part, personal and collective, the unveiling of these parasitical and manipulative influences the inorganic beings perform makes it an arduous task. People see them as their own influences, thoughts, feelings, intentions and drives. For those alien influences in our subconscious to be detected it is necessary to awaken oneself and all the functions of the mind, so that we can easily tell apart what we are, and what we are not.

One should know the nature of the thoughts. They are not our creation. Thoughts are the finest vibrations of nature, *information of the happenings in nature*, they move through space, through ether, as a grid or electromagnetic fields, similar to the electrified plasma we can see in cosmos, but in a much more delicate form. Brain is just a fine organic instrument that can get those fine vibrations, resonate, keep and combine them. As it repeats and combines vibrations that it received, the information which resembles our thoughts. Because they are not ours, thoughts can be our inspiration, as completely new information, but like demonic voices and influences that upset us and force us to go mad.[27] For the purpose of recognizing the inorganic influences it takes the awakening of the whole being, from the body to the finest actions of the mind. In such an awakened state, in the differentiation of the consciousness, lies the man's work on himself that is the uplifting of the soul. This uplifting of the soul is its lowering and grounding, so that the entire soul has all of its will in the body.

This is the reason why the inorganic beings exist: they make us become aware of ourselves in the fastest possible way. Inorganic beings are natural beings, they are just not physical. They use the fact that all the living beings consist of the natural symbiosis of

---

[27] CE-VI: Close Encounters of the Possession Kind by William J. Baldwin.

Besides the standard electroencephalography (EEG) by means of which the brain activities are registered using electrodes placed on the head, there is a new magneto encephalography (MEG) with which the activities of the brain can be registered without the contact with the head, placed nearby, close to the head, which means that the waves brain functions on extend outside of the brain.

smaller units into bigger units. They, as parasites, use the organization of the symbiosis to their advantage, for taking energy. *When the soul comes into the body it faces the same situation, that every larger unity is comprised of the smaller ones, and it is not entirely the master of its body, and with it its presence in the world, and that work and energy is being used by those who can do so. Now the soul needs to fight for the dominance over the body, to rule it in place of the parasitical entities, and when it rules the body then the entire physical surroundings transform the unconscious nature consciously making it apt for the presence of the Divine as a personality.*

If we did not have these temptations we would have no urge of becoming conscious all the way through, we would remain stuck in some phase of our growth. These temptations make us go to the whole hog, to retrieve the Divine consciousness to itself, to close the circle of the Divine emanation.

All organic and inorganic beings know this consciously or unconsciously: man on earth is designed to complete the final task of all the existence – to go back to God the Divine, to return his perfect perception to the Divine. That is the reason why all the organic and the inorganic beings force the man with such severity to become aware.

The final turning point of all the nature towards the Divine is happening on Earth, which has never happened anywhere else in the world. It happens through the man, the enlightened man.

Through enlightened man the entire manifested nature reaches its outcome and sense, all the way to the Divine from which it originally came from.

The presence of souls in the body, in the nature, affects the conformance of nature, its trans substantialization through the consciousness towards the spirit. This trans substantialization manifests as the transformation of nature and the material culture and civilization. This process, throughout the entire human history, has been achieved with pyramids built all over the world, not only that but on all the worlds where people used to live. This is the origin of the pyramids on Mars. The pyramids themselves have a characteristic of revitalizing the orgone energy[28] around themselves and

---

[28] *Orgone* is Wilhelm Reich's term for *prana* or the energy of life.

concentrating it in their centre, restoring and keeping things, the food does not go bad them, even a broken microchip placed in the centre of the pyramid can fix itself. Pyramids were built everywhere as the energy machines and the transductors of energy of the organic life into a higher form of energy. Without the pyramids organic world would just stay the same, a simple reproduction of the elementary life forms. The presence of the pyramids elevates the organization of the organic life into a higher sphere, to be adequate enough for the presence and the functioning of the consciousness. As a result, the pyramid is the most important symbol of the secret societies which control the evolution of the humankind, all the way back to Atlantis.

The same way that emanation of the Divine was happening through seven proportions, the return to the Divine through man takes place in the seven modes of existence which are represented through the seven states of consciousness and the seven chakras that are placed in a man's body. Or, to be more precise, the seven bodies of man.

Since there are incarnations of souls of the different levels of maturity or "age", and the different natures of experiences they need to go through, it is important that in this world there are different types of bodies in order to be able to undergo different types of experiences, different races and cultures, from the primitive communities to the highly developed citizen societies, and it is essential that their versatility brings forth the dynamics of the interaction among nations, and the world which will provide sufficient contents for the drama of life.

If everyone in the world were the same and equal, living in peace and harmony, the world would be like Switzerland and no development of the experience of the souls would be possible. Human souls would not be born there.

18. SOULS GET READY FOR A HUMAN LIFE BY SHAPING ALL OTHER FORMS OF LIFE

All the souls, as the monads of the Divine consciousness, participate in the creation on all levels.

The highest monads create entire universes, the planets and all the life forms on them.

All of the manifested mineral, plant and animal life does not just happen spontaneously. In the matter itself there is no information on how each of the molecules will shape, how the atoms and the molecules will join together in the symbiosis and shape a much greater organic whole. All the matter ends on the level of atoms and basic elements. They further join together by means of symbiosis. All beings, from molecules to people, have been created by the symbiosis of the smaller cells. Every cell has been consciously created using intelligent design. Because of the holographic nature of the universe every cell is conscious of itself and its function. For this reason cells can join together in the symbiosis, and with this create larger conscious wholes, such as human body, for example.[29]

Information on how to shape everything in nature comes from the outside, from the consciousness of the Divine monads or souls. They with a conscious intent, in the higher dimensions of the inorganic area, project the information field, the form of morphogenetic fields, which are used as matrix for the physical shaping of everything in the material world.

Souls are the creative designers of the entire nature, of almost all the life forms. Some forms have developed on their own, spontaneously, and those are mostly parasites and the negative forms which originate spontaneously as a consequence of the need of

---

[29] DNA does not contain information on what type of being will be formed, nor what it will do. DNA is merely a scheme of information of a protein creation. That is why people have the same number of genes as the simplest organisms. The difference is just in the different type of their organization. The patterns for all the shaping and functioning of the human beings come from the outside, from the (morphogenetic) fields. See more about this in the works of Rupert Sheldrake.

nature for the ecological balance. All the pretty shapes, that clearly display they are not a product of blind evolution because they are adorned with intelligent design which was intentional and creative, they are the product of the intent of souls. That is why the birds and the butterflies are so beautiful without any special reason for this, and flowers are carefully arranged and designed. For the nature itself it is completely unnecessary for the reasons of survival. Obviously "someone created" them. The shapes of many plants with the intelligent design of the souls are totally in accordance with their beneficial and health function. With their shape some nutritious and curative plants signify what they are good for (celery for the bones, carrots for the eyes because cut across it looks like the pupil of the eye, walnuts for the brains, grapes for the heart, etc.).

The souls design animal forms as well, through which they collect all the basic experiences of the movement and staying on in the physical world. Since animals do not possess their personality and individuality, they directly show the presence of the intelligence of souls, their intent in the forming of life. That is why animals are so sincere about everything, affectionate and dear. We recognize the purity of the presence of the intelligence of souls, although it is present in them in a very elementary form, the consciousness in them is present only on the level of moving life energy and exchanging basic information, in a smaller per cent than the one needed for the forming of the personality. Because they do not have a personality and individuality but only the pure presence of the intelligence of souls, animals can see higher dimensions, their souls are not limited to the physical body and perception that would be controlled by the mind and ego. The consciousness of the souls resides in animals after all, and sometimes this conscious soul comes to the surface, and then they seem "like people, if only they could talk", when they do something resembling the deed of a conscious being. Still, those are individual and on and off cases, of animals who live with people, so their consciousness is higher than those of the wild animals. However, our unincarnated soul ("higher self"), and the souls of our guides can sometimes act through the animals when it is necessary to help us, take the message across or save us from some danger. One should not be fooled by thinking that such deeds are done by the animals themselves because they are conscious.

In the plant and animal forms the soul is present only to a very minimal extent, barely enough for the perception of the three-dimensional physical world. In all these shapes it trains itself and prepares for the complete life in the human body, and functioning as a personality, and this provides the ecological balance for the life of man and the wealth of human experience. What would the life be without animals? Animals show to man that the conscious life is all round, that he is not the only conscious being that exists and with this they teach him the true nature of the consciousness, its omnipresence. Children, where the presence of the soul is still strong and pure, are so friendly to animals, because their souls see the presence of the soul, and for the same reason the animals are also friendly to children.

The soul becomes ready to embody itself in the physical body only after sufficient practice which means that from the higher dimensions the soul creates, by means of pure intention, shapes in the lower dimensions.

In that case its embodiment has already been prepared in its creative imagination, it has planned its body, in a certain way, and the embodied soul seems to enter consciously into its own created dream, something like the lucid dream that experiences everything here.

Soul enters the world of physical shapes with the pure intent.

It also leaves the world of shapes with the pure intent, when it reaches full consciousness of itself as the Divine outcome while it is in the body. That is what is called the enlightenment in Buddhism or the resurrection in Gnosticism and the esoteric Christianity.

It incarnates with the pure intent into the world of shapes, and from the world of illusory shapes it exits with pure intent. The way you get in is the way you get out. We will consider the exit with the intention later on. One step at a time.

19. SOUL BEING BORN IN A BODY

While discussing a soul being born in a body it is important that we emphasize a crucial fact we must always keep in mind: body is not one appearance, it consists of multiple bodies, of more dimensions, like the nature itself (earth, water, fire, air, ether), so body has several layers (Sanskrit – *kosha*): mental, emotional, energetic, astral and physical. Every one of these bodies envelops the soul and leads it to identify with the outer events in progress. Only the physical body is visible, but there is the astral one as well, we are in astral during sleep, there is the emotional, with which we feel, the energetic, with which we use energy, and the mental one we think with. According to some classifications there is the body of consciousness, the body of bliss and the nirvanic body. Discussion about them would divert us from the main topic, but their principle is clear: they are all the shells of the soul, the soul gathers experiences with them, uses them as the vehicle for moving and action. Every one of these bodies is independent of others, although they appear synchronized and united in a symbiosis. That way only the physical body, which is the roughest, resides here and now because it is connected to time the most, the bodies of feelings and mind are less dependent on time, that is why we can feel and remember what used to be, and have premonitions about things to come. Likewise, because of the independence of those bodies, we can exit with one body out of any other body: in the astral body we can leave the physical and be in astral or the mental world, or in the mental world we can be independent of the emotional and the physical. On the other hand, feelings and the mind are less aware of the illusion of time, and the physical body albeit the roughest, always stays in the only reality, here and now. Therefore, only in the physical body and during physical life presence in the highest reality can be achieved. The entire process of the man's awakening, illumination or resurrection consists of recognizing all the functions of these shells of soul, all the bodies, their symbiosis and the independence of one from another, as well as the independence of all the souls of all the other ones.

It should also be known that manipulation can take place with every body by the external influences or the inorganic beings, but not with the soul, it is also the independent, transcendental witness of all the happening. Due to the ignorance of this fact there is much confusion about the influence on man where the influences and manipulations on the physical, energetic or mental body are identified with the influences on the man's soul. Actually, the purpose of all the manipulations on man is based on forcing the man to identify only with the physical body, to be unaware of all the other bodies, other dimensions he is made of, the nature of their effect, their independence of each other as well as his own independence from them. This way a true identity of man as a soul is being forged.

Therefore, when we speak of the body, we will have in mind that body represents a multiple symbiosis of the dimensions of events, and not one thing only.

The whole nature is a holographic unity, nothing new exists in it, everything that exists in the physical, perceivable with the senses, in space and time, is merely manifested from the already existing timeless unity, the quantum field of all the possibilities, from the higher non-physical dimensions of the implicit order.

The birth of a physical body is just one conditioned, impersonal phenomenon, the process of reproduction which is in complete unity with the natural processes already present in the environment. Objectively speaking, the body is not even a phenomenon, it is in such perfect unity with the natural processes and the environmental influences that it does not stick out from the whole which constitutes it, it does not exist as an independent phenomenon.

Man is not born with the birth of the body. It is not his birth, at all. The body is just a natural phenomenon, but so perfectly suitably shaped that the soul can function through it. All the other natural phenomena, plant and animal alike, are not so fully equipped with the sense and action organs for the soul to be able to act efficiently enough as a personality and to gather the required experiences.

The experience of being born for the man happens only with the identification of the conscious soul with the unconscious, spontaneously shaped and naturally conditioned body.

The soul is a conscious witness which by its mere presence and proximity provides the meaning of life to the body.

The body, on the other hand is so perfectly shaped that all the cosmic laws are in it: the body is a microcosm. Its energy is mesmerizing for the soul which acquires experiences through it in the three-dimensional physical world.

This way the double confusion occurs which is called a man's birth: the soul due to the proximity of the body falls into oblivion of the consciousness of itself, and the body because of the presence of the soul becomes so aware that it appears it is conscious by itself. The impression "I am the body" then emerges that, both the body and the soul share.

This type of confusion lasts up until the man's final awakening or the illumination.

Souls plan their birth. They can perceive the scope of their future life from the higher dimensions, to program or insert in it some key events as the markers that will instigate the consciousness and growth in a desired direction. They do not enter life of the body by themselves either, but they are accompanied by the kindred spirits, souls as the assistants and teammates in the prearranged game of life, which get incarnated as the members of the same family, and people in the immediate surroundings, or meet each other somewhere along the life's path.

Despite planning, life seldom takes the preplanned course, because this is the universe of free will and the emanations of all the possibilities. Unexpected things happen, not only because of the conditioning of the organic world, but because the plans of one soul intersect the plans of other souls and new scenarios take place. After all, the idea of incarnation would become meaningless if it were planned and determined in its entirety, the basic purpose for the incarnation of souls would be lost, the purpose being learning from new and personal experiences.

This learning represents the learning of absolutely all experiences, both good and bad, the biggest pleasure and the worst suffering, even the ceasing of the learning itself, the decline into slavery and unconsciousness – for that is also the consequence of the free will. It is a double-edged sword. Man is free to lose the freedom. That is also a kind of experience, a very important experience, which is crucial for the consciousness of liberation.

Souls never incarnate completely, only with a smaller part. The greater part that remains unincarnated, the embodied part of the soul during the course of life experiences them as "the higher self" or "life-saving intuition", "guardian angel", and sometimes under the influence of religious programming, as "god".

Souls incarnate in the smallest percentage in the so-called "primitive people" who, even to this day, seem to live a prehistoric life. They are incapable of developing culture of living nor do they develop themselves as personalities. The soul is present in them to a degree which is necessary for maintaining life and gathering impressions through the sheer survival in the form of a human body. Since it already has experience of surviving in the lower animal bodies, it needs the rudimentary impressions of life in human bodies. People in the primitive societies have animism as the highest form of spirituality and the conviction that they are the incarnation of the animal whose totem they worship, and that they move into animals after death. Such, they can be called elementary souls, are born in civilized societies as well, as those individuals who are not capable of any higher growth, only simple work and survival.

Every soul while it is in a body has its own guide who helps it and supervises its development of life according to plan. Those are the older souls who have completed their cycle of incarnations and can help the younger ones, that is, those souls who are just starting their cycles. Sometimes it happens that the guides materialize if the situation requires it, and help save the life of the soul in a body if there is an unplanned event and the soul has been put in danger. Young souls have a bigger and a more frequent protection of the guide, whereas the older and the more experienced the souls get, the more they are on their own because they are more able to look after themselves, respectively to be in connection with its own unicarnated soul.

The soul connects the body when it is formed in the womb, a few weeks before the birth it begins to test the body occasionally, to enter it, to revive it. Expectant mothers feel it with the first movements of the child. The body itself has its own physical mind and ego. It meets the soul whilst still in the mother's womb.

The idea that the soul connects with the body at the moment of its conception is an expression of the total ignorance of the true, Divine nature of the soul, its independence of the body, and it emphasizes identification with the body and negates the soul, and is fundamentally a very materialistic viewpoint.

The very act of childbirth is not a trauma for the soul but for the body, mostly because the wrong way of giving birth which is done today under the influence of the wrong medicine. For this reason souls are usually not present during those unpleasant moments, but are waiting nearby, but the trauma of birth stays in the body that gathers all the impressions, and later on when there is a bigger identification of the soul with the body the initial trauma can affect the soul.

The death of the body, on the other hand, is so much more beautiful, the soul always experiences it as the long awaited release and the waking up from a bad dream. The soul leaves the body before the actual death of the body to avoid the agony of the dying body. In ideal circumstances it happens in a nice, painless way. The act of dying is a direct consequence of the actions during life. There are: planned, unplanned, premature, and violent deaths. Violent and unplanned death of the body always complicates the maturing of the consciousness in the body, and is, therefore, harmful.

During the first few months soul occasionally resides in the body of the child. It does this in order to get used to the body, and for the body to get used to it. Most of the time while the child is small, mostly sleeping, souls are nearby doing the research and playing. Sometimes they have to prevent the parents from making a mistake and doing something wrong.

The soul of the child joins with the soul of the mother. Hence, all the closeness and the bond between a mother and a child. That is why the mother knows "instinctively" what the child needs. They are not instincts but the connection of their souls that communicate with each other. Every young mother is filled with bliss because she is filled with the presence of one more soul, whose proximity reminds her of her own original, Divine state that she had had as a soul before birth, and which she has come to forget with the burden of life. Expectant mothers are twice richer with the presence of souls. That is why it is said they are "blessed". But because of the union of their soul with the child's soul, mothers don't just feel more happiness when the child is happy, but a bigger suffering when the child suffers.

Inarticulate conversation between a mother and a child that has not learnt to speak yet is the conversation of their souls. Mother's love in this world is the closest to God's state in which the souls reside before their birth. Because of the power of the Divine presence, the experience of appearance of a different soul through her, mothers do not want to be anything but mothers all their lives, because they feel it in that guts that it is as close as it gets to the Divine presence in this world. Mothers get more qualities spiritually from this experience, they acquire wisdom and dignity, honesty and philanthropy, regardless of education and the conditions of life and the kind of person they used to be - all mothers are alike. Fathers undergo the transformation because of the proximity of the new soul, however they did not experience this presence in their body. Their transformation is only psychological.[30] Both the father and the mother transform by mere presence of the young soul and daily monitoring of its growth in experience. Closeness and intimacy with a young, pure soul, reminds them of their own long forgotten spirituality, it restores and strengthens it. The parents get younger and revived in love with the child by their side. The transformation of the mother is complete, the woman who existed prior to all these experiences has disappeared and the new person - mother emerged. With the birth of a new being and its soul through her own being, the mother has been reborn. Proximity of the new soul has strengthened her soul in order to remind her of who she really is.

The same way that all mothers are identical because of the presence of a new soul, which enhances the presence of her Divine source, children, too are the same in this world, they are still close to the Divine source from which they came into this world. Proximity of the Divine source of the souls makes all children identical, blissful without the apparent cause, playful for the reason of existing as such. Only much later, when this source has been forgotten, when the mind becomes stronger and starts going away from the existence itself, people become individually different. However, later toward the end of life, during old age, when they, once again, get closer to the Divine source they have originated from, people become similar. All the wise old men, who have had a full life,

---

[30] This correlates with the nature of the transformation of women and men. Woman transforms completely, with dedication, all at once, and man mostly uses his mind and grows gradually in knowledge and cognition.

with no frustrations, resemble one another, they become childish, so much like the children, and they logically get along well with children, kids love them the most, because old men, like children, are so near the Divine origin of souls, this time on their way back. ("Verily I say unto you, Except ye be converted, and become as little children, ye shall not enter into the kingdom of heaven" Mathew, 18,3.)

20. THE BEGINNING OF OBLIVION

A newborn baby who has not yet begun to speak remembers its existence before birth, as a soul. Gradually, as the soul starts to adapt to the body, life energy of the body which is very strong and pure in small children, acts as the opiate on the soul, so it gives itself to the body, if for no other reason then for the sake of pleasure which this release brings. The purity of the infant, simplicity and the fact it is self-sufficient in its own existence as such, close to the soul, similar to its existence before birth and, for this reason, appealing. The more the child is cheerful and playful, the more the soul is blissful in this world, witty and playful, there is no seriousness there, the Divine existence is the game itself because it is entirely positive. The mere fact that the soul cannot act in this world through the body of a really small child that has not yet started to walk, guides it away from the body, avoiding spending too much time in it, but is usually nearby allowing the life energy of the organic world to do its job in that body, to grow, because, at this stage, there is nothing else it could do. What the soul of a child can do is influence the parents and the environment indirectly. The bliss, all older people feel in contact with the child, comes from the closeness of a new and fresh soul, which still has the complete memory of the Divine source, and refreshes this memory in those who have forgotten it.

Over a period of time souls gradually start to forget their true nature, who they are and why they were born in a body. Oblivion of the soul happens round about the time the child learns to speak. The more it learns the language of this world, the more it forgets the language of the world it came from.

Oblivion comes with the forming of speech because then the mind forms as well, more accurately the mental patterns that modulate the behavior of the consciousness. The soul is present as pure, unincarnated consciousness, the mind being a mechanism composed of various contents according to particular patterns that were shaped by the environmental influences. Those patterns then use the consciousness to modify it in its own way. Then the consciousness such as soul is also starts to forget itself, and the contents of the consciousness happening according to the prevailing mind patterns. This is how dream of a life in a body begins.

Oblivion takes place gradually, so very little children the moment they start to speak often display their knowledge of the spiritual world they came from, memory of the past lives, or insights into events only psychic people may have. They often say wise thoughts and conclusions that do not correspond with their age or maturity. But those are temporary flashes of the mind, not the consciousness that could act permanently. The process of gradual oblivion lasts until the age of six when the complete oblivion and the complete identification of the soul with the body takes over.

The complete oblivion happens for many reasons.

Firstly, the complete oblivion happens for the same reason incarnation of souls into physical body takes place: the gathering of all the experiences by participating in the drama of life. Participation is not possible without the identification, and identification is not possible without some form of oblivion.

Afterward, if the soul remembered its original state, it would never learn anything new. Likewise, it would use its previous experiences to avoid the new ones that seem unpleasant to it, and it would choose only the pleasant experiences, and the process of learning would be lost. It would not participate in the events. Total participation is necessary for the soul to learn to make its own decisions. The soul grows and matures only based on the decisions it independently makes and carries into effect, decisions that are both good and bad.

The difference from the Divine state from which it comes into this rough and limited physical world is so big that the soul would never settle for living in a body if it kept the memory of where it comes from. It would be the same as the prince living like a pauper. He could act for a while but he would not last long.

In the end, the reason why oblivion occurs is the necessity of developing one's own free will and intention, to undergo the experience of separation from the Divine and to choose, of its own accord, consciousness and will to return to the Divine. This way the Divine Absolute knows itself in the finest, most subtle, and most intimate way, through all objective knowledge and the feeling of itself.

The Divine Absolute has been reaching love through human soul since the beginning of time.

In order to reach love, all the emotions have to be lived, and all the ways of existence. Love is the very ability of overcoming certain shapes and states, consolidating the sense of all the characteristics and states of the consciousness, which is *emotional maturity that connects all differences in the light of their unity*. Without this bonding light everything would be divided, and being the way it is conflicted and lacking understanding. Hence, understanding, forgiveness and reconciliation are the beginning of love.

Love is the only thing that enables existence and harmony of everything.

Therefore, love is the other name for the Divine consciousness itself.

This is why the Divine consciousness projects itself in the form of individual souls in order to be able to heal itself and actualize in everything as love. Only this way universe can exist as the multitude of living forms. Without love there would only be the dead chaos.

That is why every child is radiant with love and brings love with its sheer existence.

21. COMMUNICATION BETWEEN MIND AND SOUL

One of the most important questions is certainly the relationship and communication of the conscious mind and subconscious soul. This relationship is filled with errors and mystifications we will try to clarify here.

In the language and in psychology the area of unconscious is called a "soul" and "the life of a soul". Additionally, the area of unconscious is far bigger and stronger than the conscious mind. It is compared with the iceberg where the visible part above the surface is far smaller than the invisible, bigger part below the water. The area of subconscious or unconscious is called a "soul" by mistake –that is merely the part of the mind which is not conscious of itself, which is split into conscious and unconscious part, that are often disharmonious. What the conscious part does not wish to know because of some unpleasant reasons, is pushed back into oblivion, into sub consciousness. However, since the subconscious is also part of the same mind, but works independently from the conscious, during the phase of reality, the conflicts are more frequent. More often than not, conflict is avoided because survival is a mutual interest, consequently a compromise occurs in the form of self-deception or with the function of lying to oneself. If the conflict is too big due to a serious trauma, the functional division of the mind happens. When this takes place spontaneously it is called schizophrenia, and when the splitting of the mind is done on purpose it becomes a programmed mind.

So, the part of the iceberg which is not visible below the surface of the conscious mind, is not "soul" nor does it constitute "the life of a soul". It is simply the bigger part of the same mind which acts consciously.

The soul is the ocean on the surface of which the whole iceberg floats.

The soul affects the whole mind, the conscious and the unconscious, always in the form of healing.

The influences of soul on the mind and life should therefore be distinguished from the unconscious influences, which can be of a split mind, repressed contents and impressions, or from the entities that have managed to inhabit such a split or programmed mind. Their influences are always either directly or indirectly negative, first displaying themselves as favorable or strikingly appealing that would later lead to the negative results and man becomes a bigger victim to the negative entities, he becomes their source of energy. Such individuals start to do misdeed by taking other people's life energy in order to feed their negative entity that possesses them via the unconscious. Or they feed the entities with their own life energy, with some obsession or vice. Since those influences come from the unconscious part of the mind, man thinks it comes from himself, that those are his misdeeds, although he feels they are stronger than him, that he does them against his will and is too weak to resist. He is weak because the conscious mind is much weaker than the unconscious. Whatever the conscious part of the mind decides, the unconscious part of the mind will make the final decision, even through deception of the conscious mind is that its will has been done. That is why the conscious mind is weaker than the unconscious, but does not want to admit it because it has a strong Ego, it adjusts to the will of the unconscious with the function of lying to itself. All the manipulations over people are based on the influences carried out on the unconscious part of the mind, and they instigate the function of lying.

If the negative influences from the subconscious mind come only from the repressed contents or impressions, then it is visible in being a slave to the habits and inability to develop the consciousness toward new possibilities, being attached to the emotional trauma, and one-sided, unbalanced behavior as a result of the blind reaction to the impressions and traumas he is a slave to.

Negative influences of the inorganic entities from the unconscious are always recognizable by imposing themselves in a pretty or an ugly way. They impose in a pretty way with voices or visions, convictions they serve to the conscious mind from the subconscious so that it thinks it is its will or "intuition". If it does not fool the man with "his intuition" in that case it represents itself in a religious context, shape or content, as "God", "angels", "Jesus", "Krishna", "Ganesh" or whichever religious pattern the man has been programmed to follow. Then the man is even more ready to listen to that rather than "his intuition". When they impose in a pretty way they are counting on the man's desires. When they are counting on the man's fears they impose in a terrible way, causing fears or scary voices or visions, in reality or sleep. They paralyze the man with fear thus forcing him into the type of behavior that suits them. The frequency of the emotion of fear in astral is the energy that feeds the negative entities. That is why the spirits frighten people, that is why devil is ugly: to frighten the man and in doing so feed on his energy. Also to disable him from seeing objectively what is going on and how to set himself free from the influences, because all objective reasoning ceases with fear around.

It is important to know that negative entities rarely affect the man by themselves, from within, from his unconscious. They use the assistance of the outer helper – some other man who is already under their influence, who works for them. They will "meet" a person who will lead them to a specific behavior that will drag them into a life which is favorable for the state of being possessed. The very physical presence, more or less intimate, may help the inorganic entity to transfer from one man to another.

True communication of the mind with soul is always healing and life-saving. It always brings true information and insight. More than anything it is the true intuition that occurs when we know with our whole being that "it is so" even though we have no proof of it. However it always rings true.

Unlike the negative entities and the split mind, influences of the soul on the conscious part are always discrete, gentle, and innocent, like a child's whisper, laughter and playing. It can be like the "inner voice", which does not sound like the voice, but is such a sudden knowing, that does not come from us, although it is clear as though it was spoken and always proves to be true. It never imposes, it is not repetitive, and it is always counting on the free will of man.

Most often soul works like that, the way we experience it is like intuition or the "inner voice". It works more often that way than we can imagine, but because of the noise and inertia of the conscious mind we rarely detect it, or later we remember that we had been given the right "warning" in such a way.

The tightness of the conscious mind makes the soul function in other ways, particularly in some special events. When the situation is such that man does not have ear for the gentle whisper, it directs events around us, which may be immediate events, but if required it may extend to several days or months.

Depending on the situation which requires some form of influence on the man, the soul directs various events, sometimes subtle and complete in both the form and the contents, like Tarkowski; sometimes it will insist on the tiniest details, like Kurosawa; if the situation is complex, it may direct scenes like Hitchcock, and when an immediate action is required, like Tarantino.

In those actions we always feel like we are a character in a theater play that someone directs live. And it is directed. Our life is a drama which was directed by our soul together with the Divine that facilitates everything. It is not the case of a soul just having directed our life in the beginning, and then entered it to fend for itself any way it knows how. Since it always comes and stays outside the time and space, the entire human life is already there, complete, it masters it from the beginning to the end. Only from the perspective of the conscious mind trapped in the illusory body of the space and time, it seems that life is unveiling slowly, following the linear time in space, and that everything is divided. It seems weird that the soul can influence events in life. Soul is present all life long, from the beginning to the end. Actually, man's whole life is in the soul, as its imagination, not outside of it.

That is why the soul can bring us a person from the other side of the world to say or do the right thing for us at just the perfect moment; take us from one situation to another in a way it all joins in the end in one big story; bring us an unknown man in the street who will tell us something or do something that will change the course of our life, so much so that he does not know why he did it, or thinks it is for some other cause; it is fun when a few people are in the game, but have no idea of their joint role in our life. Very often before we set off to see this important event we feel like "something pushed" us to go there and then.

When we do by ourselves what is in the interest of our soul or the soul of a person close to us, we feel blissful, full of positive energy, and nothing can stand in our way. Everything is going smoothly. If some activity or intention in the very beginning does not work for us, there are obstacles in our path, it is a sign that road is not in the interest of the soul. Every process in its origin has its signs, omens and indicators in the outer events that reveal its true nature, if it leads to a good or a bad outcome. Intuitive people, that is people with a stronger contact of mind with soul, can feel and detect them, and interpret them correctly.

All true creators were in the moment of creation inspired by the influence of the soul. Inspiration would come like a brainstorm, like a sudden visit of a great friend. They were able to feel the presence. When somebody pointed to the key thing in finding the solution to whatever problem they were working on, or the every-day routine, or with the help from some people, or during sleep it is all the work of the soul. Many scientific breakthroughs and works of art were discovered during sleep or immediately after waking up. Dream is also one big area that has effect of the soul on a man because he is freed of the physical limitations, but the prob-lem is that man is unconscious, it is difficult to transfer the re-ceived information to a conscious mind. It happens in another di-mension, so different from the three-dimensional physical reality, and it takes certain experience for them to be translated to the physical reality and applied practically.

Although the entire life is in the soul, and not soul in the life, the factor of free will should not be forgotten; the conscious mind in the body with experiences it has, makes its own decisions, uses this position of ostensible separation to reach the knowing of its soul, to mature separated from its essence in a body, and reach the Divine. In a man's mind, through a separated mind, the Divine, as the individual soul, it seems to observe and become aware of itself (ostensibly) outside itself. In this individual freedom the whole meaning of the life is, otherwise, life would be a film we have al-ready seen.

Because of the principle of free will, and other souls who share the same space of the physical world, the game becomes more in-tricate and many new situations arise that call for the intervention of the soul.

There are activities of the soul that are rare, but take place when life is in danger which does not go according to the original plan. Those are rescue missions, an attempt to save life so that it does not end prematurely. The effect of the soul can, in such a case, be manifested via numerous intermediaries. Those could be the souls of the deceased relatives, or people close to us, our guide, a more mature soul that supervises the events in our life and assists if necessary, and intervenes using the souls of animals. Those intermediaries can show up physically, do exactly what it takes to save our life, and then disappear. If required, they can show up as backup and advisers in critical moments. They can be like a voice that suddenly gives advice on what to do to avoid jeopardy, or to save ourselves from a dangerous situation. This voice we will hear clearly outside our head. Unfortunately, those interventions the conscious mind often misinterprets according to religious programming, as the interventions of "God" or the "Guardian Angel". Whenever it can the souls act through animals, and then we have a situation of animals saving some child or an adult in a self-sacrificing manner, with a clear intent to do so, or notify whoever of the danger someone is in. Our soul or "the higher Self" often uses animals to assert action on us, or simply to let us know we are not alone in this world, if there is no other adequate person to do this. Animals are beings with a smaller percentage of the presence of soul than the one required for the forming of a conscious personality, that is why this presence of the soul in them, although smaller, is purer and freer for the spiritual activity from the soul in a man which is prevented and obstructed by the conscious mind.

The soul in a child is purer and clearer because it does not have an obstacle of a built up mind and Ego. Therefore, children are always so dear, and they perceive the world and other people with their soul, that is why their eyes are so clear. That is why they see better and clearer.

One of the ways of soul communication with the mind is the communication of the dead with the living. The soul that has left the body and has woken up in its true nature, is perhaps, if not entirely, more awake than it was while it resided in the body, so the soul does not perceive death of a body tragically, unless the death occurred under particularly tragic circumstances. The death of a body is viewed as particularly tragic only by those individuals that stay on in the body, and are oblivious to all the higher dimensions but the physical and sensory alone. The souls who have left the body are trying to comfort the ones they left behind by sending them messages in various ways. Mostly it happens through dreams, they are the best medium for contact because they take place in astral, where the soul temporarily stays after the death of the body. If that is not enough to reach the conscious of the ones still residing in their body, then the bereaved experience a feeling of loss on the physical plain, organizing events which will with their content send a message that the "dead" one is still alive as a soul that contacts them to comfort them.

It is a completely different story of how the souls communicate with each other through people. Everything we feel as love and deep understanding towards someone, although we have not known this person for long, is actually the communication of our soul with the soul of that person. It is "Platonic love", the deepest friendship, a cordial help that was originally unsolicited, but done out of sheer human goodness. Such relationships are a lot less physical and sexual. If the lower centers are involved in this relationship, it is maintained harder, because in that case the bodily mind, Ego, prevails, and generally, it always divides and separates.

All real "human" relationships, full of love and selfless goodness and altruism are the relationships between one soul and another. That is why the body and the mind feel so good in it. They are filled with positive energy of interplay between a multitude of souls.

Every real relationship of man toward himself and others means growth in understanding and wisdom, and opening the mind to the influences of the soul, our "higher being", the Divine presence.

Every loss of this relationship, that, too, is possible in the universe of free will, is a fall into suffering and conflicts with oneself and the world. Soul in the body is a source of all good. Mind uses consciousness of soul to function in its own way. Life energy belongs to the body and receives it from the organic life. A man can live and think without the crucial influence of the soul, in suffering and ignorance.

Developing and strengthening the contact between the mind and the soul is the only thing that gives meaning to life.

That bond is the greatest inspiration for a religious life. The religious life is a subject of big manipulation of opposing forces that interfere with the relationship between a soul and a man.

Soul is always the one who communicates with the mind, and the mind is the one who most commonly has no awareness of the soul and its influences, because mostly it communicates with itself. It is understandable then why the most direct relationship between a soul and a mind happens when the mind is still, when it is completely quiet, aware and in no way impeding to the manifestation of the soul. That is the only possible way of the human uplifting in the spiritual realization.

The relationship of mind and soul is of the fundamental importance for the health of body and mind. The thing is quite simple there: the more the mind is identified with the body, the more the mind and the body are sick. The more the man is aware of himself as the transcendental soul, the more the mind and the body are healthier, more conscious, and more whole. The soul enables the whole body and mind, and it is enough just to be aware of the soul and its transcendental and essential nature, its primary significance and power and the mind will automatically become whole. All the miraculous examples of faith healing happen like this. Any health disorder and mental imbalance and clarity are lost when the consciousness of the soul is off. Every healing originates with the return of the consciousness of the soul. It is primary in everything. So if we seek health because we are ill, we won't get it, because we first think of the body, we give the primary importance to the body. That's why we got sick in the first place. We have to become fully aware of the fact that the body is merely a means of manifesting the soul, shell through which the soul shows itself, and all the dedication and attention we should devote to overcoming the body and to the soul that enables everything, the whole body. "First ask for the Kingdom of Heaven, and then you will be given everything". Those who first ask of this world, which is merely a shadow of the heavenly, will lose everything.

The direct and unmistakable personal communication of the mind and soul or higher consciousness is the practice of the consultation with I Ching, the ancient Chinese Book of Change. In the west the overall relationship with one's soul, as well as the role of soul in this life on earth is described in detail in written speeches of probably the biggest bringer of the light of soul into this world, Jesus Christ, especially in the Sermons on the Mount (Matthew 5-7), and in Gnostic gospels (*Tom's gospel* and *The Book of Tom*) where the original esoteric meaning was preserved, the way it was taught in the esoteric schools of the time (Essenes, Therapeuts,

Sufi), unlike the gospels in the Bible in which, because of the need to form an institutionalized church, changed the many words of Jesus, forged and turned them into exotic stories and parables.

22. WHY THE SOUL IS ALWAYS GOOD

The nature of the soul is the absolute good, because it is an individual expression of the Divine Absolute which enables all life, and existence itself. This individual expression is a tendency of the Divine to express itself in the best possible way, always and in all sorts of ways. The entire universe and all the life is manifested so that it can be achieved through the human soul. It is impossible for the soul to be against it in the slightest possible way. The Divine Absolute cannot be negative to itself. Then it would be neither Absolute nor the Divine.

Soul, due to its absolute nature, sees another soul in every being, sees itself in another bodily form. That is why it cannot be negative or destructive to any living being.

Soul is good because it never tries to be good – it is this way, and it cannot be different. It radiates its nature at all times.

The nature of goodness of the Divine Absolute and soul as its individual reflection should be conceived as a little more that a do-gooder. It is the Wholeness, perfection and completeness, the definition of the Absolute, everything is perfect just the way it is. There is nothing, and there can be nothing bad or wrong in the Wholeness or the Absolute. Even less so if this Absolute is Divine. If there were the smallest flaw or blemish in the Divine Absolute, it would not be able to exist, it would not be the Absolute, even less Divine.

This perfect absolute good, that sees no evil in anything, should be understood according to its proportion: it exists only in the Absolute itself, at the source of the Divine, maybe it can make it to the second proportion, in third it is barely a memory. On lower proportions, where numerous laws rule, especially on this one where the Earth is, in which the soul functions, it is not possible to confuse good or bad or reject both, because then all life can go to hell. Causality exists here the way it is. One proportion cannot be judged based on some other one. Each one has its own logic, its own set of rules. A single cell, as a part of the cosmic Holograph, is aware of the entire cosmos, but on its proportion and in its own way, and that is a different manner than the symbiosis of their consciousness in the man's body, it is aware in a different way from the galaxy which is aware in its own way. That is all one and the same consciousness, but on different proportions which, in compliance with this, form different shapes of existence. Every proportion forms its own way of living and its own logic.

The problem is that many people who practice empty philosophy on the nature of reality confuse proportions because they are not aware of them. They project the logics of one proportion onto a different proportion, then they get confused, and obsessed with their body and the physical laws, they ask the question:" Why does God allow evil?" Man who is aware of body only, not the higher dimensions and proportions, cannot be aware of the relativity of his position, nor the objective reality, and may pose a question of how good can exist even though somewhere it looks like evil.

Still, here on Earth the soul is, as a reflection of the Divine Absolute, always good, and its goodness is a distant echo of the perfection it originates from, the awareness of proportions, awareness that everything is always just good like the existence itself. Souls are not good as moralists, as the opposition to something bad, they are good like the existence is good towards everything that lives and breathes. Like the sun that shines on no matter what, soul loves the good and the sinful, the sinful one even more because it is estranged from the existence as good. The purpose of its goodness is not moral perfecting of itself or others, but the acceptance of the existence itself with the full conscious and love, the Divine existence.

Finally, the soul is always good because it strives for better, upwards, to its Divine source, where everything is absolutely good and perfect. Its basic orientation in striving upward, to perfection, is expressed as the goodness in everything it does here on Earth.

23. WHY SOME PEOPLE ARE NOT GOOD

There are two key reasons why people commit evil acts.

The first one is that those are people with young and inexperienced souls who do not possess full command of the body. This command of the body, temporarily or permanently, inorganic entities take over, and they do not have a problem to assert influence over organic beings. Those people with young souls need to acquire rough experiences, and bodies with young and inexperienced souls in pursuit of all kinds of rough experiences fall prey very easily to much older entities from the inorganic area. Those entities possess them and lead them to do deeds the souls themselves would never do. This way they help them to experience everything.

On the other hand, in regards with this, young souls seek rough and rudimentary experiences, they could ask to experience the role of a victim of some very evil act. They have to go through all experiences, both the as perpetrator and the victim. Somebody has set the stage for these experiences, the role of the victim included. This person who prepares the stage is usually a young soul that is possessed, because it, by itself, would never commit any evil act. Possession exists to fulfill such needs of a soul.

The second reason is that some human bodies do not possess the human soul, or do not have the full presence of the soul, to the full extent so that the soul makes decisions and has the last word. Soul always acts unobtrusively, it comes from the freedom and always acts according to the principle of free will and free acceptance. That is why it can happen so easily that someone "loses a soul". It will do everything to be accepted by the body, but if the other side, the body does not accept it for some reason, it will not be able to stay on.

Human bodies are just the suitable residence for the soul that nature has shaped. Sometimes, if a young and inexperienced soul should incarnate in a body, the inorganic entities may take over and completely rule over the body. Soul will remain only a passive witness till the death of a body occurs, because it never imposes by force, it does everything respecting the principle of free will, or it leaves the body which will then continue to live under the rule of the inorganic entity (demon). The initial part was important – for the soul to enter the body and start it, animate it, make it live. If it leaves the body, the body can then go on living following the biological inertia, if there is someone to keep it alive. It sometimes happens with children who have had febrile convulsions or are born mongoloid. The soul leaves and the body remains with the most basic functions, with no higher conscious or the mind. When we remember what activities a man can undertake while sleepwalking, without its conscious we are not surprised at the activities of a body with no soul. It is because a body has a mind of its own for movement and action, like animals.

In most cases the bodily mind accepts the soul because it was created for this purpose, it knows that this unifying with the soul uplifts and enriches it. There are cases, however, exceptions to the rule when there is disharmony between a body and a soul. It is hard for the soul to enter it and over a period of time there is a bigger and bigger conflict between the soul and the mind, which can turn into a destructive and deviant behavior, in its mildest form it can lead to trans sexuality and the change of sex (if the soul from the previous life was accustomed to one sex, and is now of a different sex), and in the hardest cases it can cause schizophrenia. Sometimes a soul refuses to stay with the body and then the child dies at birth. The physical cause of such a death are most commonly the vaccines (DTP – *Diphtheria, Tetanus, Pertussis)* which are full of heavy metals that cause autoimmune disorders in the form of suffocation like asthma. According to some recent surveys, especially Dr. William Torch from Medical School in Reno, The University of Nevada, all children who suffered a sudden infant death syndrome (SIDS) got their DTP vaccine several days or several weeks before the death occurred. If the baby does not die, it gets asthma or autism which is a consequence of closing a soul in, even though it stays on in the body. Sometimes a body is born and it survives without the soul, only with the physical mind, and then mongoloid children are born. Sometimes a soul decides to leave the body later, while the child is still small, if the conditions of life are unfavorable, against the circumstances of a desired life, or due to some complicated illness. Sometimes a soul leaves the body later, during adult life, and if the body survives that departure the only thing that remains is the bodily mind that possesses no capacity for any feelings or higher consciousness. It is called schizophrenia. Likewise, the case of two or three immature souls entering one body is called schizophrenia. Just for the sake of it, to try it out, to see how it works.

Possessing the body by an inorganic entity can be done by other people who are already possessed, and their name is Satanists. They have a ritual which performs this, it is called a "moon child", where the soul of a small child is suppressed or trapped and a demon inserted in place of the soul.

The soul itself may find this experience relatively interesting, since no harm can come to it, anyway. It can be constantly suppressed or pop up occasionally through the personality of man.

The man then feels like a dual personality. He feels one thing and does something else mechanically, or whatever the inorganic entity is forcing him to do. That, too, is called schizophrenia if the inorganic entity is as inexperienced as the soul.

Every man possesses the dualism of good and evil in him, of the right and wrong, conscientious action and unconscientious, which is nothing but the reflection of dualism of body and soul, an issue of predominance of soul over the body, or influences that are asserted on the body when we say that the body is possessed. The crucial bit is the percentage of the influence on the soul by the alien entities in the body. The bigger the percentage of influence of the entities the weaker the soul is, and its influence, and we call this type of person "mentally ill", "deranged", "spiritless". Language says it all. If the percentage of influence of the soul is larger in the body, it is larger in the mind, and correspondingly, the person is healthier, more soulful and emotionally more mature. Emotional maturity depends directly on the percentage of the presence and the level of decision making of the soul.

Most people with young souls, and that is majority of people on planet earth, are possessed in various ways by inorganic entities.[31]

---

[31] Their cases can be called a mental illness because they are a kind of an illness, but nothing is explained with this, except some kind of an indication of truth with this expression that there is something wrong with their soul, that it does not make decisions to a sufficient degree. There are too many cases where the cause cannot be found in the body, nor in the personal history of the individual, therefore the cause of the mental illness is obviously something that is not of this world, nor of the actual life of man. It is also said that they are split

Most people can live decently with them. Their possession can be seen mostly in their mechanical living, with some petty vice that keeps stealing their energy, which is used to feed the inorganic entity. Their possession is visible in the fact that they do not have a will of their own to release the vice and problems they create for themselves and others, they lie to themselves unconsciously, and rationalize their weaknesses while living like mediocrities.

Not all of the organic entities are negative. Most are just parasites that live off man's energy attached to his aura. It is in their best interest that the host lives so that he can feed on him. To this aim they allow their host an average spiritual and economic existence. However, only the kind of existence that would not jeopardize their survival. It is especially apparent in church goers, religious believers who would not accept any other teaching or religion. Any information that could make them aware and set them free from the possession they display strong hostility and rejection to. Conviction that only this world exists, and that there are no demons, or that only other people but themselves are possessed, is a typical mentality of such mildly possessed individuals. They get very cross when someone mentions they are possessed. They cannot explain how come they hear voices in their head, or sometimes see odd shadows and apparitions in the corner of their eyes, or in the moments between being awake and going to sleep (hypnagogia), or when in those moments they cannot move like someone sat on their chest, and they get panic stricken. They do not talk to anyone about it because they do not want to risk being called insane. It is a known fact that if they confided their experiences to a psychiatrist, they would do a lot worse than their possession. Psychiatry exists as the institutionalized support to demonize people:

---

personalities, this much is true, but all the parts are not human. They say this clearly to every psychotherapist, but he is educated not to listen to them at all. Only recently the psychotherapists have begun listening to their patients and accepting the fact they are possessed by some alien influences, as the patients have been saying all along, as the spiritual and folk tradition all over the world testifies. The pioneer work of new psychotherapy by Dr. William J. Baldwin: "Spirit Releasement Therapy: A Technical Manual" and "CE-VI: Close Encounters of the Possession Kind" are the must read for understanding the possessions we are talking about here.

all psychiatric medicines destroy the brain in such a way that demon can live in it like in heaven.

The basic method of possession inorganic entities use is to open man's perception. On the one hand, it is necessary for the entity to enter the man. On the other hand, it upsets the man because he does not know any higher dimensions and realities but the material one in which he has been maturing up until then. They achieve this partly by waking up kundalini energy in man.[32] He sees and experiences higher realities, astral appearances, has out-of-body experiences he cannot control. Having no objective knowledge of those realities, not knowing that they are as natural as this sensory world, only on different frequencies and proportions, the man is frantic and totally susceptible to all the influences. This way the inorganic entities find it easy to control him. Such a man will listen to any voice coming from them instructing him to do the most banal stupidity or crime, while in the real world he does not pay any attention to the voice of reason, and what his beloved ones are saying.

Possession is manifested in strongly emphasized identification with the contents of the mind, even though the contents do not originate from the man's mind, but have rather been planted, and man identifies with them as though they were his own.

The problem multiplies further to such an extent that there are so many possessed people that schizophrenia or madness have become a logical and natural response to the crazy world we live in.

---

[32] Kundalini energy is a name for the full energetic potential in the man's body that is numbed and that wakes up gradually as the man matures. If using some techniques kundalini wakes up suddenly to an extent higher than the man's understanding of the world and the objective knowledge he possesses, perception that is waking up like this becomes so confusing to the man that he may go insane. For this reason, an intentional waking the kundalini up is a favorite method that inorganic beings practice on a man in order to gain full control of him, on the one hand, they mix him up so he can be mentally controlled then, and on the other hand such an enhanced level of energy is ideal food for the inorganic entities. Man who has before his time woken up his kundalini uncontrollably becomes a battery for charging the inorganic entities and is very frequently placed in a soul asylum, or presents himself as the "illuminated" no one understands. In any case, he is incapable of a functional and constructive life.

The soul itself could not do anything evil or destructive, it is independent, but the energy of the human mind is the one that creates an illusion that the timeless soul is involved in time events of the nature and the body. The key role in this illusion play the energy centers of the human body – chakras. The chakra we invest energy in – is the chakra of the level of consciousness we will be. The lower the chakra identification of the soul with the activity of nature is bigger, discrepancies are bigger, and together with them the challenges in life are bigger. Identification of our transcendental spiritual essence with the body gives us the illusion that we are suffering and that we are experiencing what a normally conditioned body is experiencing. This identification would not happen nor would it be maintained if we did not invest our energy in it, particularly the three lowest chakras: sexuality, egocentricity and the will for power in the world. Such identification is created for us and is maintained by investing life energy in such lifestyles. Since we are unconscious, we do not do this consciously we have been programmed this way. The higher the chakra, the consciousness of the transcendental essence of the soul is higher, the objective insight in the nature of all the happening is clearer, our conscious of the primeval, timeless unconditionality of the soul is bigger.

The possession is always done through the lower chakras, intensifying their influence in all ways, and especially the twisted sexuality, egocentrical assertion and the will for power, but also the perverting of work of the higher chakras, twisting the true meaning of love (fourth), knowledge (fifth), insight (sixth) and the consciousness of the Divine itself (the seventh chakra*). **All those who are possessed are so in the lower chakras.** The more the man becomes aware in the right way, the more his life energy rises to higher centers and makes them actual – unless this rising is sabotaged by the inorganic entities to their advantage, by trick that this energy should be ascended by some techniques, and then the corresponding consciousness will follow. The thing works quite the opposite: energy follows the consciousness, not the reverse. If energy is ascended without the consciousness and objective knowledge, we simply get more energy to do ignorant, insane things.

Possession is always manifested in inertia and mechanical behavior in man, always in the same pattern. This physical world, life on Earth especially, is under the influence of many laws, in other

IVAN ANTIC

words, it is very inert, if we put a thing somewhere, it will stay
there until somebody moves it or it falls to pieces. It is similar with
our body, it is to a large extent prone to inertia and taking the line
of the least resistance. Inorganic forces use this fact to the maximum, they offer previously prepared patterns, recipes and techniques for all sorts of things, even enlightenment. They do almost
anything to disable free creativity which is the only foundation of
the consciousness, they disable the free will by imposing taboos
and laws that must be respected because the soul becomes stronger
with its free expressing, the expressing in freedom and self-consciousness, never by imposing or pattern. Any form of implementing the laws and regulations has only one goal – to impede the
soul.

Possession has its purpose for the soul, especially a young one,
but to the mature ones, as well. Possession practically shows the
soul how weak it is, and to what a degree it does not have its own
free will and the complete presence in a man's body. Life energy is
perfectly economical, there is not enough to waste. Energy always
goes up, or falls down, if it cannot keep, and goes there where it is
needed. The very nature of the energy is movement and happening.
It is impossible for it to stand still. Therefore, if the soul does not
use the energy given, somebody else will use it. That is why there
are inorganic entities as parasites. They practically show what the
soul did not do, but should have. Not doing what a man should do
is the same as doing wrong.

It is said that demon possesses and tempts the sinners for this
reason, that is those who have done something wrong, in the way
they live their lives. Righteous and advanced individuals demon
cannot tempt. They go for the weak and "sinners", that is the ones
who make mistakes, so that they can show them practically,
through examples, where they are making mistakes. Everyone who
wants to make headway has to "face their demons first".

Naturally, the demons themselves are not aware of their educational function on the man's soul. Maybe only their leader is aware
of this, who is one of the Divine monads who has in the dialectics
of opposites and polarity of all the Divine emanation taken on a
role that is seen as negative from our perspective.

There is a minor percentage of human bodies who live completely without the human soul. Those ones are possessed by ex-

tremely negative entities. They are the ones who commit the most ruthless crimes. We call them heartless, inhuman, and we wonder "how a man could do something like that". A man did not commit them, at least not a man with a human soul. The perpetrator is always inorganic entity that is particularly negative, also known as demon using the body of a man.[33]

It should be remembered that a man with a human soul never does any evil, it has already been said before, and every soul in another man sees another soul as itself, as the reflection of the Divine. This reflection is most apparent in children, because their souls are still fresh from the God's world they have recently come from, untainted by this world. That is why the one who does evil things to children most certainly is not of this world, it is not human, and it does not have a human soul. It is demon which in cosmic dialectics of opposites represents the opposition to souls, that are incarnated in human form in order to achieve the perfect reflection of the Divine in itself. Every aspiration in the relative world must have a counterbalance. These demons are a simple negation of all human aspirations and everything that is human. They can easily be recognized with this: they are opposed to everything that is good for people. Even the harmless astral parasites always show malice and hatred toward everything that is good, beautiful and benevolent. They even hate nice scents and adore stench. Benevolent expressions of the soul they hate the most, if nothing else they will mock and ridicule them. This opposition is easy to understand if we remind ourselves that it is all a matter of frequency, so hate is just oppositely directed frequency of love. People who are possessed by them are often destructive in their work and behavior, and the physical appearance also. They simply do not know what is right, they do not even feel it. The possessed women can be spotted relatively easily in the way they have let themselves go. Good-looking and well-behaved are only those possessed who have an important social role, such as in politics or culture, they have to keep that post in order to have an influence over other people to be

---

[33] Testimonies of people who have taken part in war battles are quite known, that in the moments of very fierce fighting people became possessed, that they did things normal man physically could not, or would not do, and that they themselves were unaware of committing them, because they were possessed.

able to demonize them. All others who are unimportant have let themselves go and are incapable of serious work. One of the most common characteristics of the demonized individual is to live at somebody else's expense, they never make an honest living. They hate work, they are incapable of work because they are incapable of responsibility and creation. Since they are parasites, they only know how to take.

Demonized people can be divided in two categories: the important and unimportant ones. The important ones participate in the demonizing of other people, and they are very skillful in social and political life. The unimportant ones are merely batteries that supply demons with life energy and are expendable, used for committing crimes, for the theft of other people's energy (by murders and violence), after which they, too, get killed.

It should be known that the cases of possessed people and "exorcism" is a show for deceiving people so that they think that it is what it really looks like. This show is performed and directed by the demonized people and their hybrids in the position of power, especially the church. They often work together, it is an arrangement, demon enters somebody, the priest comes and performs the ritual of exorcism so that the church can show and assert its power. They make movies ("Exorcist") to popularize their deception about what it looks like to be possessed, with lots of brutal and disgusting scenes. Maybe some lower demon may possess people in this fashion, in an obvious and ugly way, but the most powerful and the worst demons do not possess people like that at all. They are invisible in people, their conduct is very cunning and polite, they possess huge knowledge, they are very skillful in ruling not only a man's body they have possessed, but other people and other nations.

There is one more characteristic of demonized people, and that is the fight for power. To be in power and to glorify oneself and subjugate all others, using all people for their own selfish benefit. Man with the soul never wants to rule over other people, because he sees human soul everywhere. Since the soul is of Divine origin it does not need something so trivial like power in a mortal body in a world as low as this. Soul can only give and wish the same good like it has. Only those who do not have a soul or it is suppressed and they are not aware of it, may desire power in this world or over another man.

Bad news follows: human bodies that live without the soul[34] are in positions of the highest power in this world. Those are religious and political rulers and all the aristocracy, all owners of the corporations.[35] They have started all the wars all throughout the history, controlling both warring factions. People would never go round killing each other. A soul would never go against a soul, against itself, or against the nature they both support and develop, and corporations destroy the nature so systematically and make so many conflicts between people, chaos and instability that it is obvious people with soul would never do it. There is so much destructiveness in the world that it cannot be spontaneous, or perhaps ignorance is the real issue, for today there is knowledge and technology for people to live like in heaven. The very presence of resources and knowledge proves that all this destructiveness has been systematically planned from the highest authority and power. The existence of this much destructiveness toward nature and people is a

---

[34] They are also called organic portals, or containers. There are numerous well documented testimonies that such organic portals, containers even clones are produced and controlled by the negative aliens (reptoids, greys) in order to be able to control people and rule over them. For the documented proof and experience about this check Dr. Karla Turner's book: "Taken: Inside the Alien-Human Abduction Agenda" and "Masquerade of Angels". Also see "The Dulce Book" by Branton.

[35] That is why G. I. Gurdjieff once said that (even though people live unconscious, sleeping) sometimes it happens that people awaken spontaneously, without any real work on themselves and objective knowledge of it, and then they usually go mad when they see who really rules the world. It should be said here that there were exceptions to this world in ancient times, before our contemporary and familiar history, when people lived without the alien hybrids in power, back then the rulers were the most worthy among their people, the first among equal, and they really led their people in the best possible way. However, such ones have not been around for a long time. All the so-called "democracy" is just manipulation of the collective consciousness, in order to continue and maintain only the controlled rule of the unconscious and ignorant majority, and repress the power of the conscious minority, and "the human rights and freedoms" are nothing but the perversions.

proof that it does not come from people. No matter how unconscious and stupid, they cannot go against the survival instinct because animals could not do that either, especially in such a sophisticated way. A long time ago a trend against the survival started.

Besides possession, man is being manipulated with the mind
programming.

Programming perform those that are already possessed, the hybrids between demons and humans, to be able to spread their influence further, because it is not practical to act with possession only.
Programming enables the man to act possessed even when he is
not directly possessed. Programming becomes a way of life. *Mind
programming is based on the fact that the mind presents a system
of patterns with which the consciousness creates reality. Mind is
already a system of programs with which reality is interpreted
and created. That is the reason why it can be so easily modified
with some new programs, or "viruses" that will change, redirect,
stop, or start the programs on command.*

There is collective and individual mind programming of people.

Collective is done through religions, science, education, media,
creating the public, politics, manipulating economy, chemical influences through food and drugs, technology (microchips, and ELF
waves).

Individual is done on individuals in childhood using torture
through which the mind is split and programmed to function in a
certain way. Mind can be split into 2,197 parts maximum. Split
mind is similar to the possessed mind, because the programmed
parts behave as individual independent personalities. Today about
2% of the total population on Earth is individually programmed. In
USA alone it is about 14 million people.[36]

Man who is mechanized and programmed in some way, repeats
what he has been programmed to do, and not knowing that he has
been manipulated, he is convinced that he has of his own will did
all the deeds and misdeeds. He thinks it is reality he lives in and
cannot change, and that is why he continues to live in accordance

---

[36] Details about programming people can be found in the works of Stewart
Swerdlow who worked in Montawk military base on programming as a
programmer, mostly in his book "Blue Blood, True Blood, Conflict &
Creation".

with it. It is important here to emphasize the most crucial fact: man in whom the human soul prevails never commits evil acts and violence on other beings, nor does he deceive anyone.

By all means, life goes on with all the conspiracies, but only because it is stronger than all the attempts of destruction. No conspiracy can hinder God's plan and the nature of the emanation of consciousness and life. It can just make some local damage to some of the things in the plan. No conspiracy against people can be victorious, because people exist for Divine reasons, but they can be exposed to a lot of damage, suffering and temptation, more than necessary. To the negative entities, who are doing all the damage, it is also not in their best interest to destroy their estate, the source of food. Balance (not a very nice one) is at stake here, balance between letting people go on with their lives and having a rule over them. It is obvious that someone is interfering with human development in the fact that people have lived for thousands of years the same way, without technology, and then, suddenly in the space of about a hundred years they soared from rags to riches. A question remains if the development would have been faster and more harmonious if there had not been alien interference and obstruction.

This is the universe of free will and the manifestations of everything that can be manifested. Therefore, evil can manifest itself, but it can also be prevented. We should not overlook the existence of a systematic destruction of people just because we are still alive. A lot bigger events can take place that would cost us dearly, and only later we may become aware of why and how they happened, and what we could have done to prevent them.

For example, The First and The Second World War were planned and engineered thoroughly from one center, by Jesuits from the Vatican, they brought Hitler to power through their Catholic centre in Berlin, the book "Mein Kampf" was written by a Jesuit Straempfle, and it was assigned to Hitler, Rotshield, the bankers of Vatican, financed Hitler from his rise to power till the end of the war via The Bank of England, Rockefeller also financed and laundered his money via The New York Bank, and gave Nazis the license for producing fuel from coal to have enough fuel for the war; IBM gave them the first computer, the most state-of-the-art technology then, to process the data of the people in the concentration camp (that is why they had tattooed the numbers); after the war Joseph Mengele ended up in a military base in California as Dr. Green where he continued with his experiments till the seventies, and Hitler ended up in Argentina where he died in 1962.

What is it that you were taught in history classes?

Were you told that Stalin and Mao Zedong were educated by the Jesuits, and under their control all the time? Stalin was a Khazar[37] and his genocide conducted on the Slav People was led by The Knights of Malta and the Templars via the Khazarian banker Rothschild, who are a part of the Jesuit structure of power. Mao Zedong was under the control of the Jesuit-Masonic organization "Skulls and Bones" (a renowned educational centre for the American presidents), and his psychotic cult of personality and genocidal politics toward the Chinese people was organized by a Sidney Rittenberg.

How many million people would not have got killed then and suffered an unbelievable ordeal if these facts had been known from the start? Maybe this is a redundant question, because those that had pulled this off are still in power. You choose their people in the elections every time. This is a universe of free will.

Next example: According to the data of the Ministry of Justice in USA 450,000 children disappear yearly without a trace, they are never found, alive or dead. Every year, In India approximately a million children disappear off the face of the earth. It can hardly be called "the conspiracy theory" because this is official data. The numbers will not decrease if you stop thinking about it, or if you feel sick just by thinking about, and it seems incredible. They are likely to increase. The children are disappearing because you do not want to look at them disappearing, you cannot handle it. If you only knew that their disappearances are organized by, amongst others, the most powerful government agencies, maybe something would change, maybe you would do something except accusing "the paranoid conspiracy theorists" who "believe in aliens and demons".[38]

---

[37] Khazars converted to Judaism in the ninth century and became the Ashkenazi Jews. They spread across Europe (they became the "east European Jews") and America. Nowadays, they rule Israel. (For the history of Khazars see Arthur Koestler: *The Thirteenth Tribe*, 1976).

[38] Doing the research about the missing children and involvement of the CIA

Firstly: people with human soul could not do something like this.

Secondly: such a huge number of the missing children could not be achieved only by the demonized pedophiles and murders, even If they worked 24 hours every day of the year. Obviously, people, not even the demonized people are doing it. Some inhuman force with superior technology is taking part in it.

The presence of inorganic entities is not equally distributed across the globe, somewhere the concentration is bigger, somewhere smaller. *The criterion for the presence of evil in this world is the happiness of children.* Where the children are carefree, where they do not disappear and can walk freely in the streets, where they are freer and respected, where they are not abused legally or illegally, where the education is not twisted by the mind programming, sexualization and teaching that perversions are normal for them – there the negative entities are fewer.

One more example: How many million lives would have been saved over the conflict of Christians and Moslems, and Moslems with other nations, if people had known that the Roman Catholic church created the Islam, that it financed the Islamic conquests, that even today it controls Islam and Islamic terrorism over the Islamic secret societies and brotherhoods, that this fact is very well known in the highest circles in Islamic states, especially the ruling family in Saudi Arabia, which is of the same origin as the royal

---

and FBI in those disappearances and their creation of the satanic cults was presented very thoroughly by an ex FBI chief for Los Angeles and the west coast, Ted Gunderson. "The Finders" is one of the most important secret CIA operations against the American children that Gunderson disclosed in his research. The children are being kidnapped with the purpose of prostitution, pornography, high-tech weapons, experimental abuse, mind control, child slavery for the underground projects controlled by the aliens, white sexual slavery, and murders in satanic rituals – untold thousands of American children were kidnapped off the streets and playgrounds in America by the agents working for the CIA. "Finders" operation started in 1960's and has been kidnapping children to this day. He thinks that it is just one of the many secret crimes that are done to the American citizens by the government agents under the directives of the international Satanists collectively known as Illuminati, that control the secret or inside government of the USA, together with all the big governments anywhere in the world. After making such information public, after six attempts on his life, Ted Gunderson was poisoned in 2011.

British family Windsor (who is of German descent Saxe-Coburg and Gotha), that there are even the testimonies of Mohamed that are kept hidden away from people?

There is other evidence as big as molehills, they are not hidden, at all. The problem is that people do not see that because they are possessed in all sorts of ways. Rulers control everything, from birth, and education to work and death. They create the image for people of the world they live in, and this image is, of course, a fake so that the people do not see what is right being placed right before their noses.[39] The truth is not hidden away from people at all, it cannot be hidden, people are kept in a hypnotic state not to see it, even to accept the fake world as the real one. It is much easier this way. Afterwards they keep themselves in this phony world.

The rulers of the world have implemented mass mind control through religions and the control of knowledge. Today, New Age has started, technology makes things easier, so that the control can be achieved better by means of chemicals, various poisons in food and drugs[40], microchips in food and drugs, wrong dietary habits

---

[39] Fake image of the world or the mass mind programming started in Vatican first orchestrated by the Jesuits as ideologists. Ideas then go to London and Tavistock Institute of Human Relations, the head centre for mind control in the world, where the details of application are worked through, then to the Stanford University in USA where they are placed via Rockefeller institutions and the corresponding organizations of the United Nations, all financed and controlled by Rockefeller, ending up in all world scientific and educational institutions and text books as "the scientific truth" God given to be learnt by heart. Those that learn it by heart are given the titles of scientists, and those that advance it further, a Masonic bar called the Nobel Prize. Such falsely created image of the world is financed by the leading bankers of Vatican, Rothschild, they economically interconnect into all spheres of life via the City of London, business center of the world, and to those that, aside from all this, still have a problem to comprehend and accept these ideas, they are forced upon them by the military center, Pentagon, District of Columbia in Washington and NATO. That is why these three main centers of power in this world: Vatican, City of London and District of Columbia are completely independent and untouchable system within the system and out of reach of all international laws. While these the most powerful centers in the world are above the law and the real democratic control, there will be neither law nor real democracy in the world.

[40] Aspartame and fluoride are present everywhere, and they dumb the mind to a significant level and destroy the brain. When the newborn babies get their first vaccines full of poisons and monosodium glutamate (MSG) that damage the

totally unfit for the human beings, media exposure, extremely low frequencies (ELF) and present in every possible way through education and politics, also by the direct mass and individual mind control.

This control is done for the reasons mentioned before: if a man is not his own master, then somebody else will rule over him, there is no waste of time or energy.

People are informed in the direct way of how unconscious they are and without their own will, in an indirect way, a feeling of pressure and urgency is created of all kinds to force people to awaken and become their own masters, to start living properly which is the reason for their existence.

It is important to understand why this pressure and urgency is needed.

Soul by itself has no material interests. It can be seen in the situation when some soul achieves self-realization in the body, it automatically loses every attachment to the body and the life itself, although it is not against it. That is why it withdraws and starts living an ascetic life. It is of the Divine origin and that is why it takes a certain amount of pressure to force it into living in such a limited material body like this is, and to act in such an inferior environment.

The reason why there are influences of the negative entities on a man is in the reason that the soul itself is just pure good and it would never do anything negative and evil. That is why an outside force is needed that will introduce the negative experiences - a force that is not a soul by origin.

The soul has to go through a full spectrum of experiences of the dialectics of the opposites of nature in order to design it in its entirety, so that it would become a whole and an independent

---

neurons in the brain, followed by a series of vaccines with heavy metals that cause autoimmune disease, at the very beginning of life a weak mediocrity who is easy to control is created for life. In connection with the vaccines it should be said that the vaccination itself is one of the biggest lies and hoaxes of the modern world. Vaccination does not create immunity, and it does not protect against any diseases. It is actually used to manufacture patients. The second method of defeating people by non humans is genetically modified food (GMO), which is used to genetically modify and degenerate people.

personality while still residing in the body. Experiences of suf-fering and destructiveness are an integrated part of the dialectics of opposites on which the three-dimensional universe rests.

("Woe unto the world because of offenses! for it must needs be that offences come; but woe to that man by whom the offences cometh!" Mathew, 18,7)

On the other hand, the body itself is an impersonal process of nature and the soul is fundamentally always independent of it, no matter how identified with it the soul really is. Because of this it is possible that all bodies die, young and old, so simply and easily, because the soul does not die with them. Actually, the more the soul is present in the body, the more it has a wish to get rid of it. The problem is only in the process of awakening, whether it is fi-nalized in the body or not. If it is not, then it brings a violent end-ing of a life in a body, identification of the soul with the body did not end consciously and its learning process was disrupted. That is the only evil that happens during a violent or a premature death. That is why it is called an untimely death, the timing was off, and violent because the soul did not want for it to happen. Since the process of awakening was the reason why the soul chose to be born in a body, violent interrupting of this process is unforgivable. A lot of emotional energy, impressions and karmic patterns are invested in one life, its untimely end leads to imbalance and confusion in further studying. This confusion is intensified if there were some physical suffering as a consequence of a violent death of a body. The physical suffering as a result of violence, although it may not lead to death, equally heavily stunts the development of learning and the presence of the consciousness in the body.

With a natural or a planned death of the body the soul is ready for departure and the ceasing of the identification with the body. With a violent or an untimely death of the body the soul is caught off guard and it stays identified with the body. When it is mur-dered, it stays identified with the etheric and astral body, the copy of a physical body, and that way stays tied to the place of its physi-cal life as well as all the experiences it has not fully lived, or the ones that left the strongest impression on it, except now it is in the form of a spirit. It often deals with the circumstances of its un-timely death and the people who caused it. The souls often help find the culprit and solve the case. After a while, soul ceases to identify with the body and the bodily mind, but this happens in a much harder way.

The perpetrator of a violent crime experiences a much worse destiny than his victim. First of all, by the mere act of killing he has shown his unhealthy attachment to the body, he completely identified the person to the body so he thinks that by getting rid of the body something will be solved, which will have a very strong impact on his identification with his body and much greater suffering. With this act he also shows that he is unaware of the soul as the crucial factor in a man's existence, or rather that he is unaware of his soul, that is if he has one. Since he, with this act, ties his *karma* to the *karma* of the victim, he will have to experience everything it takes for him to realize what he had done and what kind of a damage he had inflicted upon himself and the others; since he is identified with the body and highly subjective, he will have to learn it in a very objective way: by the direct experience on his own skin of all the things he had done to others; in the end, he will have to learn that the evil he had committed was under alien influences, not of his own will, which will make it even harder for him when he realizes what he had done.

In the holographic universe, where everything is interconnected in all the dimensions, where the externality is our selfness, it is better not to go in the red, and better yet – not to make any debts, at all.

There is another big reason for this. Exiting the body, after its "death" soul leaves the time-space continuum and analyzes the entire life all at once. It recapitulates every event of its former life in the body, especially the deeds that had a particular importance for the growth of the soul, the good and the bad deeds, and even the slightest gesture of goodwill counts. As well as the slightest gesture of selfishness and denying goodness. *The consciousness is objective in this process: the soul sees and summarizes not only what it did in its body, its conscious and emotional impressions and reactions, but the impressions and reactions of all those who it did it to: how they viewed our actions. There lies the chief motivation for a new birth, for the reasons of correcting and perfecting our actions, and that is why a new birth is always voluntary*. It is fair to say that everything we do unto others we do to ourselves, and that nothing can remain hidden.

Traumas are also the experiences a soul is supposed to undergo. The difference should be noted between some experience being negative because it is violent and untimely, and when it is a need of the soul itself to go through.

We have already explained why soul has to live in the body: to accumulate with its own presence in the organic world the finest experience as existing like an individual personality that has an illusion of being separated from the Divine Absolute, and in the conditions of an ostensible separation retrieve the objective knowledge of itself and of the Divine, to be able to use this way as a road to the Divine and what is its very return to itself. With its own presence, the Divine, through its individual monads, the souls, transforms the organic world in its image to make it suitable for the reflection of the consciousness of the Divine. To make the organic world suitable for the reflection of the Divine consciousness of itself, nature's urgency and causality are not enough, nor are the laws of nature that happen mechanically and crisscross, nor the simple movement in the survival of the living beings. It takes something more, and that is the drama of the experience of life through a personal experience, through all the tragedies and comedies existence is capable of. Unlike the former simple existence, the drama of life opens opportunities for the knowing of the meaning of life. The knowing of the meaning of life through the drama of life is possible only in the personality of man, only in the heart of man all the experiences that the Divine existence can reflect may be gathered. Practicing the drama of life in all its possible shapes, contents and plots, the personality undergoes a training in order to be able to comprehend the meaning, until it finally turns to the very meaning of existence. That is why the drama of life is necessary: for the consciousness to be focused on the meaning of life. Human life is hard for this very reason, as well, because of the grandeur of the task. Souls are born in a human body to be the witnesses of the drama, because only through their testimony the human drama of existence will get the Divine realization.[41]

---

[41] A remote allusion to this process we have in the Greek myths in which the gods shared and crossed their life paths with people and being people themselves. There are a lot more accurate details which offers the Christian teaching of the embodiment of God into the man Jesus Christ. The words of

In the opposition of the good and evil that soul tempts crystallizes and focuses the personality of man, the consciousness of itself and the transcendental nature of the very soul. This is the universe of free will in which everything that is able to manifest – manifests! The presence of consciousness is strengthened of its own choice. The choice depends on observation and perception, and of the ability to tell things apart. We are here for this ability to tell things apart. It is up to us to strengthen this consciousness of distinguishing all the events and to choose rightfully, and act justly. We are free to do right and wrong, in order to see the difference and make the right choice: the one that leads to overcoming of all the oppositions, to the transcendence, not to the "right" as opposed to "wrong". If the good and evil exist together, right and wrong, it means that they are relative and dependent on each other, that they are two sides of the same medal, both should be overcome, it is unwise to opt for one side only, the other side will haunt us even more but in a secret way.

The existence of evil can be further understood as a necessary measure of the experiences which force the soul not to identify with the body too much. If life in the body in this world were just a set of pleasant experiences, it would be a trap for the soul. It would never wake up to its transcendental Divine essence. Suffering makes us awaken. Fortunately, the consciousness has always been a good counter part to the experience of suffering, and it is always, readily, available.

In order to understand how a body can be possessed, we have to understand how a symbiosis of smaller units join together to create bigger ones. Our body is a symbiosis of cells, and they are a symbiosis of atoms. Since the symbiosis like everything else in nature exists in accordance with the holographic principle, every cell is aware of itself and the wholeness to which it belongs. Since every bigger unit consists of smaller ones, everything may be divided and exist in this divided manner, bigger wholeness can be split into smaller ones. The same goes for our body and the mind it rules. Everything can be split. This fact is amply used by the inorganic

---

Jesus that have remained in the Gnostic gospels give us the most worthy details of this process and how a man can implement it successfully.

beings for the purpose of possessing. They simply use the naturally split mind, keep it that way, and increase its division.

However, although every being came about as a symbiosis it is a unique wholeness created to be functional, to stay whole, this was its original purpose, a being could not exist if it were not whole. Every child is born with previously formed organs, with eyes that have never seen light before, but immediately after birth they can see, with ears that have never listened, but can hear straight away, the whole being was born complete and ready for living. Every child is innocent and good. The wholeness which enables life is in itself good and positive. Thus it is unnatural for a child to become as abnormal and destructive as only possessed people could be. Such behavior does not make sense, therefore the cause of such a behavior lies outside humans and the human body. It is to blame "other people" and "society" because they are nothing but a group of beings like that child. If the society is not normal, then it is not normal for the same reason as the child is insane.

Therefore, the entire story of the possession gives the only logical explanation why people do things which are abnormal and against the common sense of the one who created them.

Namely, all creations of nature are united in the symbiosis and therefore separable, and nature is not only the organic physical world, it has higher dimensions, the astral world, so it is natural they have entities that form like beings in the organic world, and those astral entities can affect the organic beings, in positive and negative ways.

If science has accepted the fact that not only organic physical world exists, that there are other higher dimensions, nothing should prevent us from accepting that the principles of life extend to all the dimensions, and not just the visible physical world.

When the soul enters the body, it cannot immediately begin to rule the whole body and all its possibilities. This ruling happens gradually because the soul encounters the problem of natural division of life, and every division behind it has its own entities which exist thanks to that division. The whole process of the embodiment of the soul does not consist of one event only, the birth of the body, but rather of a series of lives during which the soul gains more strength, more power of the presence of its consciousness in the body. This presence of soul in the body grows on account of unconscious and spontaneous presence of the in-organic entities. They are reciprocal: the more there is one, the less there is another.

Any negative or destructive behavior of people is merely an indication of possession, no matter what psychological defini-tions we give it, and every positive or constructive conduct is a reflection of overcoming possession, whatever cultural definition it may be.

Physical body has three states only: either it is dead, or with a larger presence of the inorganic entities, or with a higher pres-ence of soul. When it is not dead, it can only be with a larger or a smaller presence of the consciousness of the soul or the inor-ganic entities.

If it is not accepted as such, the very notion of the soul is ne-gated. It is impossible for the soul to be negative. It means some-thing else in the body can do negative things.

Those who advocate the thesis that people are evil and capable of doing evil deeds, although deranged and insane, actually advo-cate their own ignorance of the nature of the body and the nature of the soul. Body is merely an organic set subtle enough to react to the finest frequencies of the higher dimensions.

Soul is an expression of the Divine presence in the body. Divine is the freedom that enables the existence of everything in all possi-ble ways. That is why the soul does not impose on the body as the unquestioning force, it exists as a possibility, as something that is accepted with full awareness and lived as such. Therefore, there is no soul without consciousness and goodwill. If there is not enough maturity of such a conscious that accepts the soul, but only ele-mentary awareness of survival, it is understandable that inorganic entities will find their place much easier in a body like that, be-cause they do not have a problem with their imposing, quite the opposite, it is their way of life, they always go where they can as-sert their influence. They always find their way through things by cheating and lying, because they do not have any power, whatso-ever, but unlike the soul that has Divine power, but never uses it, it always comes as consciousness and free will.

As we have stated before, all inherited experiences of the or-ganic existence through plants and animals, before they have ma-tured for the forming of the human body, have shaped certain impressions or characteristics. They behave as the little personalities, as the individual I's, like all the entities that form spontaneously. Consequently, they continue to act as the multitude of small personalities or the multitude of I's when they find themselves in a human shape. When a human soul incarnates in the body, as the complete personification of the Divine, it faces the activities of the multitude of I's in that being. *The entire human life and all the human maturing leads to understanding, designing, constituting and overcoming of all those particular characteristics or I's into one complete personality, one consciousness and one will. When that happens it is called enlightenment or the self-knowing. The word means that a person knows himself or herself, in other words it recognizes the soul for what it is independent of the body, at the same time while being in the body.* It all shows that its residing in the body is blurred by a multitude of I's experiences of the lower forms of a particular existence. Its self-knowing means that those experiences have found purpose and have become aware of a higher context and understanding, as the aspects of the existence of the nature itself, and have managed to overcome it in the context of the Divine that facilitates all.

The multitude of I's in the man facilitates the presence of the demonic entities in a man, they use this division very skillfully and maintain it in all possible ways, from astral, to the man invisible and unconscious, they imitate contents of the consciousness and the feelings, even the very thoughts that get projected in the mind, which mind accepts as its own because it does not know the origin. This is the system how they persevere in a man: man does not distinguish them from the contents of his own consciousness, his will and feelings. Those contents, naturally, create chaos and the negative states that further create the foundation for unperturbed presence and work of the inorganic entities in a man.

The division in a man is a natural phenomenon which everyone is faced with when they mean one thing and do something completely different, or do not know what they are doing, or they are so convinced that they know everything only death can stop them in what they are doing.

24. THE DECLINE OF SOUL – THE OPPOSITE POINT ON THE CIRCLE OF DIVINE MANIFESTATION

One of the most important issues of human existence is the loss of a soul, loss of oneself, which is always equal to losing the Divine presence and the final outcome is suffering. Actually, it is the biggest issue of human survival because in the scheme of the circular manifestation there is the final point, opposite of the Divine Absolute (page 51, point Omega). In order to understand the entire manifestation and circling it is imperative to understand the opposite point because it is the breaking point, the return starts right there, the ascension toward the Divine (page 51, point Alpha). Where the darkness is the biggest, there starts the turning toward the light. Therefore, it is also the point where the soul must meet its essence.

We have already said that the soul is individual manifestation of the Divine presence, that the whole existence is manifested according to the model of the holograph, that every bit represents a conscious reflection of the wholeness of the Divine. Then, the manifestation happens through a spiral decline across the proportions, with a growing number of laws which condition through the lower dimensions progressively more and more, down to the lowest material plain, which represents a concrete personification and compilation of all the other dimensions. The obvious conclusion is that only there, in the organic world, it is possible to form a conscious subject who will be aware of all the other dimensions and proportions, and the entire manifestation: which is the man. In man's self-conscious happens the most perfect reflection of the Divine and the meaning of all the emanation. The mirror of consciousness is the clearest there so that nothing exists in it but the reflection of the one who is, what is, the reality itself. The Divine Absolute is the only reality.

Mirror is merely a clean surface. The soul of the man is the same, it is not just some entity, some special core of something that travels through the dimensions doing something. Soul is the clean surface of the Divine presence, clean space that enables everything. The fact is that the Divine enables the very space that enables everything. That is why it can be described as the emptiness, no other way. Soul is also the void through which the Divine Absolute can express itself. A relative mind cannot conceive that, because it always moves in relationships and deals with contents, therefore it pictures the emptiness always in a negative context, as the absence of something. That is why it is said that it is paradoxal to the mind, that it is transcendental, above dualism. The Divine emptiness is above dualism of empty and full. It facilitates them both, it enables all the contradictions. It is the absolute positivism, the absolute good.

Only the blank void that enables everything can enable the consciousness. As the void the consciousness facilitates everything, enlightens, brings to the light of the day the existence itself, all the opposites, only consciousness can be aware of the opposites, while the mind is always busy with one aspect and content. It needs logic and conclusion in order to comprehend something. Consciousness merely enlightens things as they are. The mind uses consciousness for its work, same as the lamp uses electric energy. Lamp is the mind, and invisible, omnipresent electric energy is the consciousness. When the mind is not conscious it just uses the invisible, omnipresent consciousness in its work, perception and understanding, then the virtual entity known as Ego thinks that it shines all by itself. It is in that case always unaware of the completeness, the consciousness as such and it thinks that it is special, self-sufficient and an independent self-existing wholeness. This imagination first took place with the Son, the third reflection of the Divine, and from then on it continued to repeat itself in the lower and lower proportions, making lower and denser creations. The manifestation of the cosmos is identical to the manifestation of the Ego in man for this very reason. With the disappearance of Ego the manifested universe disappears, and only the Divine as the only reality remains as the man's Self.

Ego is the farthest point opposing the Divine (page 51, point Omega). It is the virtual end point the Divine projected to see itself from the outside, objectively, from the observation point of an individual being that is aware of itself, that has a mind, and can understand the world, but thinks that he is separated from the

Divine Wholeness, that it is separate, and alone. It is identified with the illusory material shape of its existence, with the body, to a point where he thinks there is no God, or that he exists and can be talked to and negotiated with like with a salesman. That was the whole point of the entire virtual manifestation of the Divine as objective existence, of the entire universe.

In that final state, in the state of egoism separation and alienation provide the hardest drama, the biggest suffering, the most intimate confronting of the existence. Suffering in that state consists of the fact that all virtual manifestation looks so real there, it looks the most dense, existence is least visible the way it really is, as the virtual manifestation of the consciousness of the Divine, its imagination; it looks like dead matter here real in itself. Hell looks real here.

To lead itself to that final point, opposite of itself, the Divine had to involve forces to help, inorganic beings that do not have a soul as the reflection of itself, but only the aspiration toward shaping and survival in any shape, way or form. Those are demonic entities that use the higher dimensions of the inorganic world and astral for its shaping, and because all they really care about is to exists at all costs, they do not care about esthetics (that is why they are ugly) nor ethics, nor any other kind of existence. That is why they are evil and heartless. Their blind aspiration for survival is much stronger than the interest of keeping a soul in the body, that is why their power to possess the bodies is so big and omnipresent. Soul stays in the body following the principle of free will, not the struggle for survival. For this reason man loses his soul and free will so easily under the influence of inorganic entities.

Soul does not want to be in the body, at all. It resides in the body merely for the purpose of bringing the awakening to the end point of the Divine manifestation, to the human body, mind and ego, and providing the turning point toward the source, the return to the Divine. Therefore the returning to the Divine always displays the supremacy of soul over the body, mind and ego.

The Divine had to involve those blind demonic forces of survival in order to provide its souls a virtual experience of the most opposite point, of utter alienation of the Divine omnipresence, the dead matter in the clash of opposites, the fight for survival in the body, in the separated consciousness of the mind, in Ego. *Soul would never be able to reach this state, the experience of the final point of its own accord, because it always has awareness of itself, of its Divine essence. That is why it needs help.*

The nature of the circle – and circle is the nature of the Divine – is the transformation, turning point that starts in the opposite point, the return to the starting point, toward the source, the beginning, to the Divine.

What is the way that demonic beings manage to keep the man in the opposite point of the biggest darkness and alienation of the mind? In the way that they have convinced him the mind is real in itself, they guide him toward identifying with the mind, with certain contents, the way they appear in his mind, and then it all looks real by itself, separate, and everything seems material. They have installed their mind to the man which is aware only of shapes and formations, not the consciousness that enables both the mind, and the shaping of everything. For this reason human mind can be possessed by demons, because it has their nature. Demons are the greatest masters of the mind. They invented it. Identification with the mind blocks the consciousness which facilitates it. It is an unconscious state, but it can act because it has life energy and uses the consciousness, but unconsciously. The consciousness, that originates from the very Divine, relies on the freedom so much that we can use it without being aware of the fact that we are using it. In the same manner we can use the mind all our lives, to work and survive, and never be aware of the consciousness that that enables the mind and all the living. By using the consciousness received because of the proximity of the soul, the mind has convinced itself that it itself is conscious too, and that its consciousness is all that can be had of the consciousness.

That is why we use the mind in such a subjective way, and are unaware of the Divine consciousness that facilitates the mind and the existence itself, we have the experience of suffering and conflict with the world, the nature and other people, because they use the mind in the same way as us.

If the Divine is absolute, which means that nothing is possible outside of it and that it is everything, the illusion of being separated from the Divine Absolute is possible only in the mind, *it can only be imagined*, it is not for real. Only the thought has that freedom and ability to imagine that it is special, outside the Absolute.

On this freedom its creativity is based. When the whole structure of the mind is persuaded by this, it becomes Ego, a virtual alienated individual. For this reason only the awakening is needed for us to know that we are one with the Divine, that is why the self-knowing of man is also the knowing of God. *That is why the inorganic beings can affect only such mind structure in an attempt to imagine the impossible.* That is why it is said that they have installed our mind, and that is a different way of saying that the ability of the mind to think is an impossibility, that a special individual is outside the realm of the Divine Absolute, the most important effect of the inorganic beings is guiding the soul through the illusion of alienation, through the opposition of the Divine presence.

The return to the Divine begins by awakening the mind, by the knowing that mind merely uses the consciousness that is infinitely larger than itself, and not the fact that the mind creates the consciousness. By doing so the consciousness in a man becomes objective. Soul starts to be present in the body to a higher degree, it represses the power of the inorganic entities, it becomes present like the empty space that facilitates the consciousness of the Divine itself.

The awaking of the mind begins with the knowledge that the mind does not exist independently, that it is virtual reality, same as matter. That is why in science and metaphysics the reality of matter and mind is discovered simultaneously. Quantum physics developed at the same time when the deep psychology did. Mind is but a collection of thoughts, and thoughts are the finest vibrations of nature, events on the level of frequencies or information. There is not some mind that thinks. There are merely thoughts as information being acquired and designed in one place.

Mind is not a notion but an event. The notion has its essence, events are only processes in action. A notion is like a stone, an event is like a wave – it exists but has no essence. A wave is just an event between the wind and the ocean, a process, an appearance.

Mind is like a process that resembles a wave or a river, it does not possess the essence within. If it had its essence it could not be lost. If it did not have its essence, it could disappear without a trace. It sometimes happens in deep sleep.

Mind is just a process. Actually, there is no mind – merely the thoughts that move at such speed that they appear to exist in continuity. One thought arrives, then another thought follows, and another, and another, and so forth. The space between them is so tiny that a break between two thoughts is invisible. This way all thoughts seem merged together, they become continuity, and because of this continuity man seems to think that mind really exists.

Thoughts exist – but not to the mind that thinks. The same way the electrons exist – but there is no matter as such. The thought is the electron of the mind.

When mind is carefully brought to awakening, it disappears. Only the consciousness remains. Mind with thoughts is like the cloud, and the consciousness is the sky. The clouds are constantly going by, the sky always remains. The clouds may take a short break in the man, to compose themselves and shape, even cause the storm and the thunder, but move on and the man stays aware of himself still, like the sky which is always clear above the clouds. *The consciousness in man is the space where the clouds travel, where the thoughts can be aware of its nature, to convey information of the events. The man's soul is this consciousness which always remains, like the sky, that enables everything, the empty space that reveals everything, the body and the thoughts and the world.*

When with the awareness mind as an imaginary subject disappears, as Ego which seems to do things all by itself, which thinks, then we see that thoughts only go through us, that we are the empty space, that no thought is our own. Thought has no thoughts, soul does not think, they are just the presence of the consciousness that reveals and facilitates. Thinking is the process of designing something. Souls do not think because they know everything already. That is why they can use thoughts as the exchange of information, but they, themselves, do not produce any thoughts. They already are everything that the thoughts point out to and are trying to imagine and design. Soul is a wholeness which can use thoughts as its components, but cannot be reduced to them. Soul is outside the mind, and thoughts are always in the mind.

The other parable that can help us explain the relation between the mind and soul is a wheel or a circle and its centre. Circle or the rim of the wheel is superficial, manifested consciousness we have when we are awake, in everyday conscious mind or Ego. The wheel keeps on turning, one moment it is in the point which is up, and then we are in an elevated state of consciousness, positive and awake, the next moment we are down, when the wheel of fortune keeps trampling us over, when we feel the full weight of the wheel of *karma*. The centre of the circle or wheel is the immovable soul or Self (Self, *atman* in *advaita vedanta*). From that centre the entire circle is available, the whole *karma* and the whole life. Only from this centre we see the way things truly are, the whole circle of existence, flawless and without the thoughts that remain on the rim, from that point on we see the true nature of everything we look at, understand everything that is happening. It defines the expression "transcending the mind": leaving the rim which is always in motion (mind) and transition to the immobile centre (Self). From the edge, from the mind or Ego, our knowing is always just partial, depending on the information that is available – from its center, the Self or soul, we always see the complete as it is, with no information.

The more the soul is present in man, the degree to which we are centered in it (in self), the more the mind is (seemingly) as a real entity absent. The more the soul is absent, meaning us being displaced from the centre, the more the illusion of the mind rules, or, the mind with all its illusions.

More accurately, the inorganic entities that support the illusions of the mind rule.

The basic mechanism by means of which the inorganic entities maintain the illusions of the mind, is the illusion that mind exists on its own, and together with it the Ego, a separate individual. That is why they are doing their best to convince the man that the mind is real in itself and should be controlled in every possible way.

Firstly, based on the illusion of Ego they convince the man that he does everything of his own will. Since this doing due to subjectivity and the lack of consciousness is not so good, then they induce a strong feeling of guilt and impurity for "the done deeds". This they implement by using the Judeo-Christian religions. This feeling of guilt further strengthens the mind into Ego, as well as the separation and fear. Separation and fear create conflicts between people and a general war. Both fear and suffering are frequencies used for feeding the inorganic beings. In this manner people go round in circles. It is necessary for them to persuade the man that he is the one who does everything of his own will, and therefore is responsible for the consequences, and that mind is real, that the mind is his, that it creates all the thoughts. For this reason they are developing various ethical and religious ways of mind control. Nowadays, they extend it further to the New Age teachings of assorted subtle ways of mind control and "emotional cleansing". *Every form of handling the mind, conscious or unconscious, is a confirmation that mind as such exists, that Ego exists, the one who has a mind and deals with it. Every confirmation and emphasizing the existence of the mind and Ego produce the unconscious as a result. This unconscious then really affects the mind and Ego even stronger. The amount of reality we choose to give our mind and Ego becomes a real impact of the unconscious on the mind and Ego. It is a never ending story of the virtual division of reality or the matrix we live in. It is the foundation of the demonism which has been sophisticated and scientifically well-developed better than ever before.*

Mind is impossible to control because there is no mind to begin with, nor is there Ego, that will control it. One virtual reality can be controlled with another virtual reality in order to produce the true reality. The tendency to control the mind is a closed circle of self preservation of the illusion of mind and Ego. This leads to the further splitting of the mind. Mind is the one who has a mind, Ego, they keep each other in an illusory survival. All contents of the mind and emotional traumas that Ego safeguards for the sake of its own survival , do not objectively exist on their own, so they are impossible to cleanse by means of some form of control or effort. They are made instantly for the purpose of using the mind as such, with the illusion of the Ego which is created by that aspiration. The contents of the mind and emotional trauma are equally virtual as the one who owns them. *The more we consider ourselves to be a separate entity, the more contents of the mind and emotions seem real to us, as separate entities. That is a mutual reflection. All the memories and all the suffering we carry with us all our lives is but a wrong focus of the consciousness on the mind, Ego and the illusion of time which they create. They are created instantly when the mind projects them. They do not exist or last as objects, that is why it is impossible to remove them as objects. They ap-*

pear and disappear instantly with the mind, or in deep sleep with no dreams or in enlightenment, when there is no mind just pure existence.

Consciousness is the one that rescues from this closed circle, the consciousness of oneself as the empty space, void that enables the entire existence, all the illusions of mind and Ego cease to exist.

Soul in a man begins to overcome the mind and the body when it knows all the emptiness of the mind and all the illusions it creates – and mind creates all the illusions of setting the mind free, as though it were real by itself; all the methods of releasement from the Ego, as though it were real by itself; all the methods of releasement of emotional traumas and suffering as though they were real by themselves. *Soul in a man strengthens as empty space, free void, the presence of the Divine. It is therefore said that his presence is a testimony.* It is simply there all the time, conscious all the time. Therefore, it is said that it is transcendental, independent of all the events and time. Consequently, this empty space we experience as our essence, our Self, is our soul. That is exactly what it is.

In this pure consciousness of the Self we should get stuck and stay there with no hesitation and no mental doings, with the complete stillness of the entire being, body and mind. By ceasing and numbing. That is awakening. There is nothing one should do before that, before the awakening. For as long as we think there is something we should do first before awakening, even to facilitate the awakening, we are sleeping, prolonging the sleep.

In other words, *there is nothing we should do to reverse the return of the circular manifestation of the Divine from its furthermost point of alienation in manifesting the world. We should just stop manifesting further in imagination for it to return to itself. We should stop creating the world further in imagination because there is nothing to create, the conscious subject is the end of creation, of all the manifestation, everything pours into it and reaches its purpose, the consciousness of itself. Aside from the conscious subject only an illusion can exist.*

When the man reaches the consciousness of itself, its Self, when he disappears as an individual, wholeness of the Divine Absolute is finalized. The soul has returned to its outcome.

25. SOME OF THE CHARACTERISTICS AND PROBLEMS OF YOUNG SOULS

It is hard to describe the problems young souls encounter in this world, for them it is certainly the hardest, but more than anyone else they have the biggest protection by the guide.

First of all, it should be understood that young souls are not merely born in primitive societies, nor are they mentally retarded people. We have already said that the soul does not incarnate in its entirety. People in primitive communities are most often animated by the smaller percentage of the consciousness of the souls, less than necessary for the forming of the complete personality, barely sufficient to give them life. That is why they do not have a developed *karma* or the drama of life, their life is usually based on physical survival. Young souls with a real incarnation are born side by side the developed ones, in the conditions where they can form a personality and go through all the karmic plots of the drama of life. Actually, young souls get more often born near the more developed souls, in conditions where they will be able to learn easier and receive tutoring.

Their problems boil down to the previously mentioned problem of being possessed by the inorganic entities, and to their basic immaturity, meaning the emotional and intellectual immaturity, inability to comprehend things by insight, but only through the direct, live experience.

Only the bodies that have young and immature souls can be possessed, because physically the mind is naturally split and lacking objectivity, and the souls themselves are too inexperienced to prevent the organic entities from interfering and affecting the psycho energetic events of the body. Possession of their body is a reflection of their inability to have their own will and to have a complete personality. Unless the man has power over himself, the others will have power over him.

Young souls are those who have to go through every single experience by themselves in order to understand the greatest good and the worst evil and suffering. That is exactly what they want, nobody can divert them from going down the path of bad experiences they are heading toward, and advice given by the older soul is to no effect. They often protest because they find the intervention as imposing on their "will" and jeopardizing their "freedom". Their biggest success is not repeating their mistakes too often, managing to learn something in the process, if the bad experience does not push them to even worse experiences. Young souls want to go through all the experiences because they know that only with complete understanding of the drama of life in all the aspects and all the roles may bring further maturity and growth. Growth and maturing of souls counts only what they have learnt themselves based on the decisions they made themselves.

The biggest difficulty for young souls presents lack of understanding of others for their young temperament, emotional immaturity, which is not evil, but simply being young and inexperienced. Unfortunately, because of this lack of understanding they suffer the most. Especially because of other immature souls. They have a need to experience everything to the maximum, negative experiences also, which makes them look stupid, although they are not, they just have a need to know various stupid things, that also constitute life, and during this process they mature.

Young souls always mean well, because they are like children, but because of lack of experience they often react improperly, but always completely sincerely. When, for example, they criticize a member of the family they usually do not choose words, kind-heartedly supposing that everyone would have the understanding, because their sincerity is so apparent. It would be apparent to an older soul, but if he goes for an equally young soul, lack of understanding and conflict are inevitable. Their kind-hearted negativity has its compensation in the kind-hearted positivism, ready to forgive it all and give themselves and others a second chance. They are not exclusive and vindictive (unless they are possessed).

Lack of understanding and conflicts among people always happen only amongst young souls who are equally immature. If one soul is older and more mature, reconciliation and understanding usually follow.[42]

---

[42] The smarter one will yield.

Only the demonized bodies of young souls cause conflicts and violence. Those are often those souls that wish to go through the negative experiences, those that they experience on their own skin and those they put other people through. Young souls themselves are not violent, but they are susceptible to being possessed by the negative entities and mistakes, so they are violent for this reason, and they themselves are the biggest victims of the evil deeds they commit. Every soul matures over a period of time and realizes that some form of repentance is needed for all the negative things it has done.

Immaturity of young souls clearly shows that they do not have an objective and true insight into the facts and arguments. That is their main reason for the conflicts with other people. All their maturing consists of being lead to perceive and deduce correctly, not to think they are right because that is how it looks to them based on their previous knowledge and experience. This leading has to be performed discretely, in an indirect way, their actions should never be called out directly wrong or immature. Young souls can never accept the fact that they are young and immature, they react fiercely to such suggestions. Life and work with the immature souls is often particularly hard and strenuous, especially because life tragedies are a part of their lessons.

One of the biggest problems of young souls is their inability to see how immature they really are and as a consequence they imagine themselves to be more mature than they are, and they become conceited. That is the pride that all spiritual teachings emphasize as the biggest obstacle to growth and maturing. Arrogance is a naive tendency toward correctness and sublimity, but without reaching this aim. It is all fancied, imagined.

That and all the other problems of young souls rest on the law of the level of consciousness people have. According to this law the one who is on a lower level of consciousness never sees the one who is on a higher level, they can only see the ones who resemble them or on the level lower than them. To anyone who is on a higher level of consciousness than his own, he thinks that he is on a lower level than him, for everyone who is more awakened than him, he thinks that he is sleeping, for anyone who is more normal than him he thinks that he is "deranged" in some way. Naturally, for those who are on a lower level of consciousness than him, he tends to humiliate them. It is a naive way to give oneself credit.

Positive experiences constitute their growth. Young souls are the real children of this world, those are people who most rejoice life, song and dance, who adorn and bring cheer and joy into this world. Their identification with the body brings the greatest passion and life, sensual pleasures, beauty and love. Only thanks to them this world is pretty and cheerful.

Being a parent and raising a child, being a witness of their growth and learning during which process the parent learns as well, is one of the most important practices young souls face thanks to which they learn and mature themselves. Parenthood is their most important school. Unfortunately, because of their immaturity it is often an arduous task for them and their children alike. That is why many older souls decide to be born as the children to the young souls. Then those older souls, as their children, help them grow and mature. Souls grow the best in an atmosphere of love and understanding.

The most important issue with the young souls is understanding that they have a need to experience all things and all the possibilities, although it looks like stupid behavior; it is not stupidity it is a way of learning. It is important to know that young souls deal more with the outside world and experiences in the world, than with their own being, changing and perfecting themselves. They react to the outside world much more than dealing with the challenges creatively. Temptations and contents of the world are too strong and too fascinating for them. Identification with the contents of the world is far stronger than the objectivity and independence.

The soul cannot learn by learning stuff by heart, but with the very way of its existence, by moving and acting through all the states of consciousness, going through all the experiences and all the opposites life has to offer.

By doing so the soul learns how to be free: if everything is possible, the worst evil and the greatest good, then everything is free already. If it were not in its essence already, it never could become. It will observe one day and it will be free one day in this world. It will understand that it is the essence of the world. If the world shows it that it is the freedom that enables all, then freedom is its own nature, there is no outside world. It there were, it is there as a reflection of the self-knowing of the soul.

26. SOME OF THE CHARACTERISTICS AND PROBLEMS OF THE MEDIUM DEVELOPED SOULS

Their emphasis is on the development and on more complex issues. While the young souls are mostly coached on rough and simple experiences of good and evil, pleasure and pain, souls that are medium developed go into more subtle and complex relationships and the contents of such experiences in order to be able to design them on a higher level and give them meaning. Those are the souls that become creative in some way. They start, for the first time to turn inward, toward themselves, they begin to be aware of the processes regarding their own maturing, trying out their powers of action more not just a spontaneous responding like the young souls do. This way they gradually begin to work on themselves and to get rid of the external influences.

Those are the good and hardworking people who build their life, professional success and family patiently, who create new things, design the ones already in existence and by doing so they improve life and knowledge.

One thing which is apparent is a growing absence of possession by the inorganic entities, they appear healthy and prudent. Too often a subtle influence of mental programs that condition people can be seen on them, usually in the form of religious teaching and abiding by the law and order in the form of authority. This is actually useful and necessary because people in that phase of development need some authority as a director and leader, and religious programs contain many useful instructions as well as inspiration for the higher knowledge.

The whole point of development of medium developed souls is the thing that they have started to release themselves from the influence of the inorganic entities and to increase the presence of their own consciousness in the body.

They start some kind of work on themselves, that is what is generally known as "spirituality" or esoteric knowledge. Most of them are still in a naive, exoteric phase, where they stick to some form of religious or scientific teachings. Most of the medium developed souls develop science or religion, or they improve the social relations. Minority among them, the advanced ones, move on into the higher phase when they get to know the esoteric meanings of various exoteric stories and myths, when they start to apply the truth to themselves.

The essence of their work on themselves matches the diminishing of splitting of their personality into multiple I's, being possessed by alien influences, inorganic entities, and the ever growing unity of their consciousness of themselves, also the forming of one I or the complete personality, the forming of one magnetic centre, aim and idea which is in the process of growing and leading them to an ever growing awakening. Immature people with split personalities do not have one goal, a magnetic centre, but are inconsistent and changeable and that is why they do not achieve much, nor do they change and improve themselves.

Soul truly begins to grow in the body when a man has one magnetic centre or the goal of development, and that is the consciousness of himself as the outcome of all life.

27. SOME CHARACTERISTICS AND PROBLEMS OF HIGHLY DEVELOPED SOULS

Highly developed souls are the ones who have achieved a rule over the body, who are masters of the body and can no longer fall prey to the inorganic entities or be fascinated by the experience of the physical world.

They are wise men among people. But they are not the recognized sages that people bow to like they do to saints or gurus. Only very few people have taken on that role as the true teachers and masters, because it is in line with the time and circumstances and they were expected to do so, to spread inspiration, the consciousness and understanding among people, and they are teachers in this world. Their maturing during youth is not in learning, but recognizing the knowledge they already have in them. They do not learn from the books, they merely recognize their knowledge in the books. They see things as they are, they do not need any additional explanation, maybe a little reminding and tuning in with the time and the language of the environment they live in. They unmistakably know which is which, they recognize every truth and deception. It is because of the maturity of the soul in them. Emotional maturity depends only of the maturity of the soul in a man. Soul sees everything because it is one with the universal Field that consolidates everything, therefore it knows everything.

Such people are often psychic, or clairvoyant. If an unknown person comes to them for the first time, they immediately see what the person is like, because they are "plugged in" the universal Field that everything seemingly separated joins into one.

On this planet Earth a smaller percentage of highly developed souls is born. The ones that are born, do that out of need to help and maintain a proper development of life and to learn to be patient with immature and young souls, in order to become better teachers. Soul goes back to the Divine only in the human form and after it has known all the dramas of life. In cosmos there are many planets like this, theaters for rehearsing the life dramas, and this planet is a theater for children, because on Earth mainly young souls are born. That is why it is fairly easy to notice who is a puppet on the world stage, and who rules and pulls the strings behind the scene, who Illuminati are, and who the working class. It is not concealed at all, like in Japanese Burnaku Theater.

Majority of highly developed souls, masters, come to us in the form of unknown and humble people, from modest families and smaller places, where the conditions are good, mostly to help a great soul develop further, or to help a *Bringer of the light*[43] come to earth. They do not deal with world issues, nor are they out there to save the world. They merely deal with the issues of great individuals, other great souls and aid them discretely in developing and making their mark on the world. If a great soul that is going to change the world is about to be born, nearby a highly developed soul will be to assist, as a formal or informal teacher, a friend or a member of the family.

Their influence is discrete because of their maturity, only immature people brag about their actions. The mature ones know that it is not them who act but the Divine emanation is the only one that acts in everything.

The highly developed souls have finished their cycle of incarnations and they are not born because it is a biological imperative, but out of mercy to assist the growth. They are totally committed to the reason of their living so they do not consider having their own offspring as important, unless it is tied to their purpose, and the reason for their action. They are characterized by their modesty, the lack of addiction of any kind, especially sensual, the total commitment toward rightness and goodness. It is impossible for them to imagine any evil or injustice, let alone commit it. They sincerely pity the one who does evil deeds, even if he is doing it to them. They do not hold grudges against anyone because they are aware of the context in which things happen, they know that the Divine wholeness is doing everything, and not some individual, that people do evil things because they lack awareness of themselves and the wider context of happenings, and all their effort is aimed at increasing awareness in people. Forgiveness and love

---

[43] On this topic it is necessary to read the Barbara Marciniak book: *Bringers of the Dawn*. The next chapter will deal with this further.

stem from the consciousness of the wholeness. The more the soul is mature in the body, the more objective consciousness it has of itself and the wholeness and compassion.

Their voice is especially soft and kind-hearted, they always say exactly what should be said, their advice is always wise, true, far-reaching and unobtrusive. They use uncomplicated speech and sayings.

They are always in a positive mood, full of forgiveness and inspiration they emit on the others.

In this world there is no better person but them to learn the meaning of the unconditional Divine love from, and to feel its living presence.

There is nothing in this world that can unhinge them and make them go off the right path and the consciousness they have of themselves.

28. SOME OF THE OBSERVATIONS OF THE YOUNG, MEDIUM AND THE HIGHLY DEVELOPED SOULS

Young, medium, and highly developed souls are basically identical, there are no differences among the souls. All souls are fundamentally the emanation of the Divine consciousness of itself, only subjectively they are experienced as individual, because of the relativity of space and time in which the Divine consciousness is manifested. However, in this relative world there are differences, it is based on distinguishing, therefore the souls that manifest themselves on this proportion, in the conditioned and relative space and time, seem different, some appear to be young and immature, and others as old and mature. It is happening for a simple reason to bring to consciousness all the options of existence, they should all be experienced differently, which is possible only here in such a relative world like this is and the manifestations of differences.

That is why we speak of the souls of different level of maturity. It is due to the urgency of this relative world, and not because of the souls themselves.

This relative world we live in is real in its proportion and its laws must be respected while we are in it. That is why there is the reality of life the way it is, and all the differences between the people and nations.

This being the relative reality makes the difference between the "age" of the souls relative. That what is above every relativity is consciousness, that is why we can be aware of relativity. Consciousness is outside the realms of time and space, it illuminates them all, that is why we can be aware of space and time. The presence of consciousness is the factor which determines the state of one soul in the relative world, and whether it is "young" or "old", "mature" or "immature". That is why the advancement of the soul is relative, its expressing in the existence depends on the presence of the consciousness in it, its consciousness. One soul can grow from young to very mature and advanced in the course of merely one incarnation. It is not necessary for it to go through several incarnations on the same level of maturity. Everything is free to develop as it sees fit, everything is relative and depends on the crystallization of the consciousness which is the reason why the soul incarnates on this plain: *because of rehearsing to keep the presence of the consciousness in all the states and experiences on Earth. The more the soul manages to keep the objective consciousness in the body, the more mature it is.*

The method of learning is different with the souls of different maturity.

Young souls have yet to go through all the experiences the consciousness of the experiences will provide. For this reason it is hard for them to think abstractly, to recognize and predict some facts and situations ahead. Any attempt to alert them to this is usually in vain. Because of the need to learn from all experiences, young souls equally have a need for the negative experiences, the ones they put themselves through and the ones they put others through.

Medium developed souls have gone through enough rough experiences to be able to think critically and foresee things, to apply in reality what they have learnt from experiences in order to improve the conditions of living in the future. Those are the people who are able to comprehend the received information, to learn from them and to apply what they have learnt without the rough experience. Those are educated people who spread the progressive culture of living. However, their knowledge depends on the information that have reached them and the ones they are able to understand. They have not entirely gone through all the rough experiences although they are largely on a good way of overcoming them. The need for negative experiences is a lot smaller, certainly a lot smaller for putting other people through their personal hell, although they still suffer because of the earlier mistakes and wrongdoings. The advancement of the culture of living consists of overcoming and designing experiences, in minimizing doing the negative deeds to other people.

Highly developed souls have completely gone through the rough experiences and they do not have a need to learn from them. Their knowledge does not depend on the information that reach them. They know already, and the information is only to remind them of the facts they know. All the information they deal with only remove the oblivion every soul has while coming into this world. Even in the most miserable living conditions they look like an elite among people, but they are always modest even if they are wealthy. They never put other people through negative experiences, they are always positive and full of love, and if they endure some hardship it is merely to set an example, to show others the way, to teach them something.

Souls of various degrees of maturity also gather experiences in certain nations and on certain locations. Those locations are determined by geography, and souls are determined by a certain level of maturity and the genetics of the body they inhabit.

In some nations the souls of special maturity incarnate, and then we see the mentality of certain nations, some are advanced and some are backward. However, material wealth does not reflect the maturity of the souls, quite the contrary, more mature souls do not depend on material wealth and they do not want it, more immature souls depend on it and they seek it because they tend to compensate with outer means their own inadequacies and their lack of ability to buy what they do not have and what they are not, they want to satisfy their illusions with material pleasures. Young and immature souls are more tied to material illusions and that is why they show inclination toward them. That is why young souls show two ways of living: the most immature ones live in primitive conditions because they are incapable of higher development and effort, they try to realize their life goals using violent means, or they cannot achieve them anyhow, and a little more advanced young souls live in extreme luxury and wealth with which they attempt to satisfy their illusions. With the outside wealth and the sophisticated organization of life they try to make up for what they have not achieved within themselves. For example, the tendency for peace and tranquility they cannot attain because this is a characteristic of very mature souls, their inner state of maturity as the independence of the external influence. That is why young souls try to satisfy this need by living on their islands. Their relationships they cannot be realized on the foundation of true understanding, maturity and love, so they base their relationships on material conditions and make up for the lack of inner qualities by imitation.

It is a general rule that the young and the immature souls get incarnated in similar environment that will provide them with the rough experience they themselves do not possess. Of course, the rough experiences can be experienced anywhere else in the world, in the civilized environment as well as the primitive ones, but most are concentrated in environments where the rough experiences prevail and where they can take place.

The most advanced souls have concentrated themselves on certain locations because it was the only way for them to develop civilization and culture. Urban civilization is the chief generator of culture, because all activities of people and the flows of consciousness are acquired there, intercrossing and concentrating. It must be concentrated on certain favorable places and well-organized. If all the advanced souls were born equally, all over the world, scattered, they could never get themselves organized in to the development of civilization.

In such environments the destructive influence was much less present, people lived nicer and more peacefully, children were happy and carefree, people cordial and kind, soulful. The environments of ancient Slavs used to be such. Lately, some Slavic countries resemble this model.

In earlier times the presence of the locations where the advanced souls dwell was more conspicuous, and the civilizations flourished, and where immature souls live, there were the locations where primitive human specimens were born with the minimum presence of soul, or without it, who do nothing but survival and animal struggle for life.

Nowadays those locations are mixed, on the one hand it is good because the possibilities for growth for the young souls are better, but on the other hand it has its bad sides because the ones without the soul have been given the opportunity to move to civilized parts of the world and continue with their rampage.

Nations with little or no presence of soul are known as conquerors, they usually commit a genocide on the conquered nations and destroy everything that is not their own imposing their own rule.

In earlier times there was a possibility for them to be stopped by wars, today they have received visas and even have possibility to travel everywhere without visas and migrate wherever they like.

It is done deliberately by the rulers over people, the Illuminati, they stimulate multiculturalism to stifle the middle class, intelligentsia and the bigger concentration of consciousness and culture in civilized parts by means of violence and chaos people with primitive mentality bring into their environment. Multiculturism really does enrich cultures, but it also destroys them, it creates an undefined chaos which can only be regulated by imposing bigger control by the government. It is exactly the thing that suits the rulers perfectly: the more control, the better. For that reason they create more violence in order to have an excuse to implement more authority and control.

Instead of imposing multiculturism as the only way of enriching cultures, which in reality leads to degeneration, a truly beneficial thing would be to develop the advanced cultures and civilizations that would appreciate, understand and advance other cultures and human communities. They naturally become beacons to all people when the advanced souls that inhabit them develop them in a proper way.

The negative inorganic entities are well under way of preventing such a proper development of culture by the advanced souls, they spread the authority of immature and possessed people, they call their rule "democracy", and perversions "human rights and freedoms".

29. EVERYDAY LIFE OF BRINGERS OF THE LIGHT

Bringers of the light are souls that bring light and knowledge. They have an ancient organization, one ancient society, ancient spiritual bond based on which they perform a certain task in a certain stellar system. Members of this elite organization come to Earth in different times to do their job. This usually happens when one cycle is set and when the events are perfect for them to allow the energy from higher space and the energy of Earth blend within their own being. Energies from space always arrive on Earth, and energies from Earth always rise to space. The mankind is building a bridge between heaven and Earth which some people call the "rainbow bridge". The Bringers of Light allow for those energies to blend with them so the dawning that is the light awakens in them. By doing so they bring this dawning to the civilization. Through themselves they ground and transform the cosmic consciousness on Earth and advance the evolution of consciousness. Just by being present on Earth, not with any extraordinary effort. External work, physical and mental, belongs to the lower developed souls.

Bringers of the Light are the original souls of the first people that have remained in the Divine consciousness and have never gone astray from it. They stayed pure and perfect emanations of the Divine, one with the Divine. It was necessary for them as such to be able to go down among the souls that are incarnating, who with this act transform the lowest, material nature. They need the help of these original souls because here they are like in a prison, in oblivion. In order to set themselves free they need some outside help of those who are already free and awake, in other words, somebody who already has objective knowledge of the liberation and the freedom itself. If all the souls were in this prison of matrix, they would never be able to set themselves free if they did not have some outside help. Bringers of the Light are, therefore, those that bring the necessary help from the outside. This is what they always do: when some planetary system with souls becomes closed too much, due to the opposing influence of the inorganic entities, they break it up from within.

Inorganic entities of the negative orientation are especially alert in connection with them. They do whatever it takes to prevent their awakening. For the Bringers of the Light have a process of awakening in the body, although much easier and quicker, similar to the very advanced souls, it is enough for them to recognize information not to learn it as new. However, the inorganic entities cannot harm them in any way, apart from sabotaging them in various ways taking their energy with various temptations, counting on the fact that their time for action will pass.

Bringers of the Dawn are those great souls, known or unknown who have turned the wheels of civilization with their actions and teachings, but more than anything with their unobtrusive presence. The ones we know were great founders of religions and teachings that have redirected the human civilization and the development of consciousness on higher levels. Their actions are always inconspicuous and based on the development of the free will of souls, and never imposing the "real truths". Free will as the basis for the consciousness of souls is the only "right" thing for them. Therefore when we say that they were founders of the great teachings and religions, we do not mean the ones that were based and spread with violence and dictatorship, like Islam for example, on lies and cheating, like the Roman Catholic church (which created Islam for the purpose of destroying the mystery schools of Gnostics and Sufis, and the free will of the advanced souls). We have in mind the perfect systems of self-development such as Patanjali's system of yoga, the original Taoism of Lao Tzu, the original Buddhism of Siddhartha Gautama, the early Christian teaching, Gnosticism and Sufism that spread on their own, just by being true and helping the development of the consciousness of people, never by imposing.

Bringers have different roles, they do not merely bring religious teachings, but they act in other ways as well, some of them bring the scientific and technical revolution. One of them Nikola Tesla, brought light to the whole world, eliminated the dark that had been around for centuries, and practically provided or pointed toward the discoveries that will advance the mankind for centuries to come.

Even more powerful are the unknown Bringers of the Light who often live very humbly and insensibly in this world, as witnesses, but with their own presence enable the presence of the Divine. They are very hard to recognize because they conceal themselves so well acting the role of an ordinary man, that if someone pointed him out in your neighborhood, you would never believe it. If they are not doing anything important at the moment, and are not under a big attack of the inorganic beings, they can be recognized by the objective knowledge they always spread around them, condensed as the essence of various forms of knowledge, the oldest and the latest, in a more or less discreet way, and the nutty, Divine humor that always comes from them. To them wits and witty is the same.

30. PLANETS CONDITION THE ORGANIC WORLD

Having already discussed the proportions of the Divine manifestation, we have said that they manifest with geometric progression to even bigger conditionality, down to the organic life on Earth. They take place by means of spiral rotation: from the spiral rotation of the cluster of galaxies, revolution of the stars in galaxies, the revolving of planets around the stars, to revolving the satellites around those planets. The process ends in appearance of the organic world on the planets and the conscious subject who is aware of this entire process, the entire manifestation of the Divine. Only in it all the manifestation ends and returns to the Divine.

The whole process is mechanical, but accidental as well, because it lies on the freedom of manifesting anything that can be manifested. If it were not all mechanized, the consciousness in nature would not be possible. If everything were accidental, everything would be chaotic and the cosmos would not exist, and the consciousness would not be needed.

The organic world and the appearance of man who has the potential of being conscious is the place where the shift of manifesting the Divine happens, from mechanical complexity to the conscious designing and the creative knowledge of oneself. It happens on the planets with organic life like planet Earth. They always happen in some spiral motion: from the spiral revolution of the clusters of galaxies, revolution of stars in the galaxies, revolving the planets around the stars, to the revolving of the satellites around those planets. The process ends in the appearance of the organic life on planets and the conscious subject who is aware of this entire process, the entire manifestation of the Divine. The finalization of manifestation ends in him and returns to the Divine. The entire process is mechanical, but also accidental, because it is based on the freedom to manifest everything that can be manifested. If everything were mechanical, consciousness as such would not be able to manifest in nature. If it all were accidental, everything would be chaotic and cosmos would not exist, so the consciousness would not be needed. The organic world and the appearance of man who can be aware is the place where the turning point of the emanation of the Divine takes place, from the mechanical complexity to the conscious design and creative Self-knowledge. It happens on the planets with the organic life such as Earth is. Human body shaped there first with all the sense and action organs. It became suitable for the presence of the conscious emanations of the Divine as a soul. The presence of the soul in the body gradually perfected with the fight against the mechanicalness of the nature and external conditioning, both organic and inorganic factors, against the inertia of nature to form spontaneously, mechanically, and when it reaches sufficient strength of the presence, the process turns upward returning to the Divine. Since everything is a holograph, this Divine is not outside the being, it is within. The return of the Divine to itself does not happen outside the man but within him, as his self-knowing. Man is a microcosm, therefore the higher dimensions are in him, not outside of him.

In order for this turnover to take place, from the unconscious mechanicalness of the natural shaping to the conscious self-knowing, the very unconsciousness and mechanicalness must be known, as the already existing state. The understanding of the existing state is the commencement of the consciousness. Man is as conscious as he is aware of the fact how unconscious he is, and he becomes as free as he comes to realize to what a degree he lacks freedom.

Let us take it one step at a time: everything is mechanical and conditioned here.

All life on this planet is completely conditioned by the outside planetary factors, by other planets. Cosmos is actually an energetic phenomenon, it is manifested as the electric energy in the physical dimension, on the material plain. The entire cosmos is electric plasma, all the stars are this as well, and gravity is nothing other than an electrostatic phenomenon, but on different proportions. On the proportion of the atom it is atomic energy, on the proportion of the molecule and cells it is life energy, on the proportion of the planets it is gravity. All the visible material universe is created from the invisible higher dimensions, the highest one being ether or *akasha*. It manifests from the Divine as empty void that contains and enables everything that can exist. In the manifested universe the empty void exists as "Black holes", and it enables the appearance of all the material elements. That is why they have the strongest gravitational pull, everything comes out of them, and everything comes into them: simultaneously, because linear time does not exist there.

All planets are electromagnetic wholes, they are moved by magnetic induction by the external influences, other planets and stars, and affect with their own magnetic induction smaller wholes and other planets. Magnetic induction on favorable places moves the complexity of a higher order from the simple moving of the planets, and it moves the organic life. It is the life on Earth as we know it. It is completely conditioned with the magnetic induction of the movement of the surrounding planets, as well as the movement of planet Earth around the sun and other planets. The magnetic inductor that is the closest to Earth is the Moon. It most strongly affects organic life. While the Earth circulates around the sun, it gets life from the sun, but because the Moon goes round the Earth, it attracts all the life energy of Earth toward itself.

We can see this in biological cycles and the rhythms of living beings, not just the tides, but everything grows with the growing of the moon, and declines with the waning of the Moon. Moon does not merely affect the physical body and the cells, but the energetic body as well. It affects the mood swings and it affects the mind as well (hence *lunatic*).

Other planets affect all the existing life, each in its own way.

The story is just beginning: they are not influences on the physical and biological processes, but on events also.

Somebody lied to us and told us to draw the line and set the boundaries, a differentiation, between our body, its spontaneous internal biological processes seeing clearly in them the conditionality and thinking that was natural – and that what the body does on the outside is considered "our free will"?

Such boundaries in cosmos do not exist.

There is nothing that is just external, or anything that is just internal, everything that is outside is inside as well.

Our mind conditioned by the Moon and egotistic subjectivity is the fraud that is convincing us that boundaries do exist, that the skin is the border which separates the natural necessity from "our free will", and that what happens in the body, all the metabolic processes, are "natural" and as such spontaneous, and what we do with the same body on the outside is "our free will" and "intention". Beyond that illusion of the mind, reality is that the degree of our ability to influence our autonomous nervous system, heart beats, is reciprocal to influencing our actions in the outside world. It is equally conditioned, but seems different to us because the Ego that decides on the whole matter is placed somewhere in between, it divides everything into its own and the outsider's, the same way into the external and internal, to what it does and what it does not do. If it admitted to itself that everything is equally conditioned then it itself would also have to be conditioned, and it would not find justification for its existence. This way it can create an illusion that it decides on certain matters and that it is the basis for its existence. It is all due to the very nature of perception, our senses are turned outside of the body and that is what we exchange that what is in the body with that what is outside. A common optical illusion, but with the far-reaching consequences.

What contributes to this illusion is the fact that the conditionality of the biological processes in the body and conditionality of the outside events take place on different proportions. The known biochemical processes function inside the body, and outside the body, in the events of destiny, causality functions on higher proportions. The science of Astrology shows them in detail. The most apparent example is the effect of the cardinal points in horoscope, the Ascendant, the middle of the sky (MC), IC, and the Descendent. If somebody was born at noon, Sun will be in his ninth or tenth house, near MC, such a person will have a strong aspiration or destiny to be focused on its career, traveling, politics and issues of importance to the society and public life. Details on how to achieve this are entirely up to the person, but the destiny of life orientation has already been mapped out for him or her. If somebody was born around midnight, his Sun is going to be in the fourth house and he will be, quite the contrary, attached to home and family, tradition, he will be inclined to lead a quiet life far away from the public eye. Details of how he will do it are up to his character and the temperament, which other factors of the horoscope indicate, but the most dominant aspiration will be the already mentioned attachment to home and his origin. Those who were born at sunset will have a strong seventh house and to them marriage and the matters of public will be of utmost importance, the influence of others and the relationship with others. Once again, the details do not matter, how a person will realize its plan, but his destiny will generally be like that. If the ruler of the fourth house is in twelfth, the person in question will lose assets and real estate. It does not matter how he does it, although it can be seen with a detailed analysis of the horoscope. If the planets in the seventh house are afflicted, such a person will either not enter matrimony, or will have a bad experience in marriage. It concerns only the part of the day when someone was born. The season also determines the temperament and the character of every person. Everyone can see the difference between people who were born in winter and in summer, spring or fall. Fall and winter months produce individuals who are deeper and more stable, more serious than spring and summer signs, which on the other hand produce individuals who show more joy of life and like to deal with the issues in the outside world. The nature then manifests itself and everything is booming, while in fall and winter nature goes back to itself and it is cold on the outside. People who were born in these seasons also display similar characteristics. Always changeable and unique positions of the planets give a unique complexity to every man, therefore even with the planetary conditionality, the part of the day (ascendant) and season (sun sign), everyone can express themselves and grow in a unique way. But because of this complexity we should not overlook the general conditionality of it all.

So, the external influences refer to the general direction. They are like the field of influence. This field is our boundary, like the railings. In this cage of existence we are free to fidget as we please, but we have to be in it. For example, we are conditioned with the process of feeding, it is irrelevant how we come to the food, we can even use our free will and creativity here, but we are conditioned with the feeding itself as a sphere of influence which acts as limitation.

External conditionality we do not see just because we are dealing with different proportions of one and the same conditionality. Biological processes are known in a body, and outside the body the planetary influences. They are much bigger and they function differently. We can freely wiggle in them as we see fit, but we cannot exit the sphere of their influence and the flow of their functioning.

Mind should have its will and intention, since it already exists like that, because it is a reflection of the consciousness, but does anyone remember when this crucial transition happened, from the unconscious living in all the natural activities, to the conscious decisions and personal will?

It has not happened since the day we were born. We can only imagine it, same as with everything else. We first did something, and then later we proclaimed this act our free and conscious will.

Every movement of our body we have ever made in our lives we made under the external influences of the Moon, Sun and other planets. Moon most of all. Other planets affect other aspects of events, character and temperament.[44] We are a part of that machine. It is natural. The same way cells in our body are connected in one unit that functions and they do not function by themselves but as the whole, our body too, is a part of the whole of the cosmos it belongs to. If the movement of all the planets and the Earth stopped, the induction of life energy would stop as well and our body would stop, our heart would stop, we would fall and disintegrate into dust. In any case, life as we know it would be different, we could not live like this, without some kind of artificial help like during the cosmic flights, where you can go on living, because the whole cosmos is filled with magnetic induction of the celestial bodies, but not like on Earth.

We have yet to get out of that machine, to gain our consciousness and our will, to make a conscious differentiation which will truly set us free, not only in the imagination like it has been till now. The work on oneself is what it is all about.

However, the fact that you are reading about it means that not everything is conditioned and mechanical, that the lid is not fully closed on the pot. There is an impulse of the consciousness above, souls of the finest Divine emanation bring it. It manifests in the man as the mind, as the common consciousness in a real state, but in a young man it is sleeping, it functions to the point that he knows what to do and that he is able to learn. This principle which

---

[44] The science of Astrology explains these influences accurately. See more on this topic in my book "The Meta-physics of Astrology".

is potentially present in every human being must gain strength more and more, for the presence of the consciousness is enabled in the body and the whole life of man, so it can survive in all circumstances and all the states. Practicing consciousness to remain present in all the states of the body and mind is the practice of meditation.

The presence of a soul in the body is so powerful that it gives the unconscious mind an illusory impression that it acts of its own free will, that it is conscious all by itself although it is not, that the body moves and acts independently of the environment.

It is a necessary deception of every presence of the soul. The same way that the proximity of the magnet moves metal shavings, like the transparent crystal placed on a colored surface looks colored, the presence of the soul, which gives consciousness, looks like the mind itself is conscious and that it consciously and independently rules the body.

The strengthening of consciousness in the body is called work on oneself or the meditation. With this work on oneself the insight into the difference between the consciousness of the mind and of the body strengthens. It always represents the fight against inertia and the natural mechanicalness, against the gravity of the external influences, and against the identification with the mind and the body. Only with the work on oneself a real conscious differentiation is created that will set us free. Up until that moment only a differentiation in the mind which equals sleep existed, because we have the same mind when we sleep. You can see that for yourself: you think all day long, you have your inner dialogue, but you think in sleep as well, dream is but a three-dimensional thinking, one complex we ponder all day long, becomes a 3D drama, the same thoughts continue when you wake up in the morning. We use the same mind for thinking when we are awake and when we sleep.

The true distinguishing and differentiation from every type of conditionality happens when we learn to distinguish ourselves from our soul, mind and body. Only a differentiation like that can produce the objective consciousness or awareness.

31. SOUL AND KARMA

If all organic world we live in is conditioned, if only a fraction of the mind is conscious enough to be able to learn and make a difference by working on itself and strengthening the presence of the consciousness, how can we explain all the changes a man causes around himself and in nature? When a man works in the world, when he does whatever and achieves some results and consequences that have a feedback effect on him, how does this happen?

Soul is always independent of the body, it is always just a witness.

The presence of soul gives consciousness to the mind and body.

The consciousness is of the Divine origin and that is why it is the best attractor of the appearances. Appearances exist because there is the reflection of the consciousness, as we saw it in the beginning.

Consciousness in the body is individualized, limited to the horizon within the reach of its senses and personal experiences. It does not do or create anything new, but only from the whole of all the possibilities causes to become manifested that what is within its horizon of experience. When the individual consciousness matures enough for some experience, it appears from the universal field in the horizon of its experience. Mind is the activator of the appearances, through the mind the potential actualizes into actual, the unmanifested into manifested. For this reason it is said that mind is the vanguard of all the appearances, that the mind is the creator, etc. Mind does not create, because there is no creation, merely manifesting, but the manifestation looks like creation, as though the mind designed and did something new. It looks as though it were new only to the subject it shows itself to.

The consciousness of the soul in the body is the cause of appearance of the body itself and all the circumstances in which that body exists, moves and seemingly acts.

The experimental physics has proved this. Subatomic particles in the experiment act as the wave of energy and at the same time as particles, too, because they are basically quantum fluctuation. How they will act depends on the presence of the observer in the experiment. When a man, the observer is present, they act as particles, as a material appearance, and when there is no observer, then it is the energy wave, the pure potential. Recent scientific studies have shown that this type of behavior is not reserved for the sub-atomic particles, but also to large molecules (fullerene, C60). They exist only when observed. Otherwise, they are just a field of pure energy.

The same thing was stated long ago in the teaching of *sankhya*, that the nature knows it is being observed by people and acts as the material shape in the form of particles. This is dealt with in the classical texts of *sankhya* (*Sankhya karika* 59, and *Sankhya sutra* III.69) where it was said that nature is like the dancer showing its dance before an observer and retrieving when it gets known.

The same thing is taught in Gnostic teachings when they claim that God through man continues the creation of the world, that that is the reason for sending souls into matter in order to ennoble and save all the beings. Hence the myth of Jesus as the son of God, that is God that embodies in a human body in order to save the world, to become a man through Jesus, and through Christ man becomes God.

That is the journey of souls being described here.

The consciousness of souls through a man's mind actualizes all the appearing matter into actual existence.

This actualization that individual consciousness through the mind does looks like work a man does. Indirectly, through the body, the presence of the soul affects the surrounding nature, for it to transform from a simple survival state to events of the higher order, to culture, science, technology and civilization. This looks like the man built it. It happens automatically, man is merely the means.

Man's illusion is man thinking that he is doing something. This imagining is what is called Ego-mind. The Divine Whole is doing it all. The only thing a man can really do is to work on himself with the aim of awakening the ancient independence of the soul as the personification of the Divine Whole. There is nothing else a man can do in this world. That is the very reason why he exists in this world. Everything else he does, all the culture and science, is an indirect consequence and serves the purpose of this work for the soul.

According to the words of Bhagavan Sri Ramana Maharshi, man's true measure and grandeur starts where he as an individual ceases to exist. In other words, when in this world he starts to exist as the living soul.

All true spiritual traditions teach that man has two births, one natural, bodily, and the other one spiritual or the birth of the soul, Divine. Without the "second birth" in the free will and consciousness it was regarded, for a reason, that man does not exist as the "real man", because the birth of his physical body does not differ in any way from other reproductive processes in nature – which are characterized by transience, decay, and dying of everything that is born (John, 3:3-7).

From such a fundamental distinguishing, the experience of transcendence, all the great religions and ethics originated. Due to the necessity of the second birth there is religiousness and spirituality, therefore the necessity produced all the human culture, whose general sense is overcoming the unconscious natural conditionality and time. Therefore, it is overcoming death. The whole life of a religious man is the process of being born in the Spirit. This differentiation has always pointed toward man being authentic only in the spiritual freedom that overcomes the passing of being and time, that is how he can only exist. Only when he is unaware of his spiritual authenticity the man suffers death, transience and suffering. It can be overcome with self-knowing. The fundamental significance of the "second birth" is best described by the Gnostic vision of the bird that is coming out of the egg which represents the cosmos. In order for the man to be truly born again and become he has to pierce the shell of the naturally given world the same way bird pierces the egg, starts flying of its own will and only then begins to exist. The man's natural, biological birth is similar to the forming of the egg, he is "born" but that is not the final act, his biological birth is only a possibility for the other, true spiritual birth, same as the bird, the symbol of spirit has yet to come out of the egg with its own effort.[45]

---

[45] According to the Gnostic version Herman Hesse brought to life for us in "Demian": The bird is piercing the egg. The egg is the world. Those who want to be born, must destroy a world. The bird flies to god. God's name is *Abraxas*. (*Abraxas* is the deity that unifies, transcends all the opposites, allusion to the

The second adequate comparison can be with the seed and the tree. Man is with his biological birth like the seed that has tree in itself. It has to fall apart for it to produce a tree that would sprout and bear many fruits. If it does not change, it will just rot. If it wants to preserve itself, it will be lost. If it gives itself away, it will get a true life. In the same natural way man in which he originated, closed within his subjectivity, he must disappear in the transformation of the spiritual growth for it to explore his true potential, to be manifested for what objectively he is. This is the whole idea of resurrection.

If the process of becoming were finished, if we really existed with our natural origin, we could never become aware of ourselves nor would existence become a personal experience through awakening. Nothing new would happen. The personality would not be possible. It would continue to be a process of natural determination and we would be no different from the animals.

The essential human becomes only with the transcendence of the natural conditioning.

If that is work, if nature does it all, what are karma and destiny?

Transformation of the entire nature happens twofold.

First: as the universal appearance due to the very presence of consciousness in the form of individual souls.

Second: the presence of consciousness through the souls is limited with the body, the mind and its subjectivity.

Subjectivity is needed for the existence to be lived to the full, and it creates all the versatility of experiences we see as individual destinies. Because of the freedom of manifesting everything that can be manifested, activities can take place in all possible ways. Since everything is connected in the universal Field, all deeds are interconnected.

Namely, in the experimental physics the following has been discovered: when one particle splits into two parts, and those parts are separated several kilometers apart, when one part is affected somehow, with the change of its frequency for example, the other part, although distant, will react simultaneously like the part that has been affected, like they are still connected in one particle. This shows that the seeming separation does not separate the matter at

transcendence of the mind.)

all, because all the visible parts are basically one same energy field. All is one. The same thing was discovered about DNA. If a sample of the DNA of one man is taken and placed several kilometers apart, and then the DNA is affected in a man, the part which is removed will react simultaneously as though it were still present in the man, as though it were affected, although it did not happen. Actually, it will react a little sooner like it has a premonition.

This way it is not all matter that is connected into one, but all the doings in the matter as well. The Universal Field doesn't connect only all the energy, but all the doings. Movement and doings produce consequences that are inseparable from the subject that moves them, and then brings them in existence in any possible way. Those consequences are called karman, which means act, deed, but also the consequences of a certain action. The meaning of karman as the action and the consequence of the actions, indicates the field that connects everything, the one who acts and the actions themselves, and their consequences.

Subjectivity is the basis for karma and it shows us yet another aspect of it. All the experiences that a soul experiences in the body it attracted itself to be able to experience them, but soul isn't alone in this world, there are many souls with their needs for experiences. The cafe is full and it works 24 hours. Add to which, there are no rules, everything is allowed. That is why there is karma we have created ourselves, and the one somebody imposed on us. There are experiences we attract and the experiences we put others through because they attracted them. Also there are experiences we didn't ask for and neither did the others. It is not only our karma that works but also somebody else's. The law of gravity is at work or might is right, like the influence of the planets in free cosmos, stronger gravity will beat the weaker one. If we live with somebody whose negative karma is stronger than our positive, we won't do so well with him. We will have to put up with somebody else's karma. It often is a bigger problem than solving our own karma.

Understanding that there is an influence of other people's karma, we should also realize that their karma is also a part of our karma. There are souls that have incarnated just to help us learn some lesson we are incapable of learning. They can play a positive role, a teacher who teaches us in a nice way, but a negative as well, depending on the lesson and our capacity to learn. Sometimes it is necessary for us to be taught in a harder way, through negative experiences. Such a way of learning provide, besides the inorganic entities, other souls who inflict seeming pain and suffering for us, that make us feel hard in life, those are the persons we hate the most and can't stand, but who play an important role in our life and we can't avoid them. Repulsion we feel for them comes from the obvious fact that these persons hit where it hurts, they touch the soft spots we don't see and don't want to change. Very often those are great souls who help us in the most important way, but in this world they deliberately have a hard and ungrateful destiny of enabling us to reach the most important lessons we ourselves would never want to learn. Unlike people who are demonized by the negative entities, these souls would never do us any serious harm. In time we will conclude that they actually prevented us from slipping into evil, that they taught us in an indirect way, but because of our immaturity their deeds looked like negative doings on us.

We have already said that everything is a holograph, every tiny bit mimics the whole. All the higher and more subtle dimensions, that precede the visible reality, aren't outside, but within the man, they constitute a man, but are unaware of him, and his mind. It is the area of the individual and collective unconscious.

This practically means, in regards to the issue of karma, that all the subtle happenings on the outside reflect the man on the inside, as the contents of his unconscious, as the more shallow or the deeper impressions, *vassana* and *samskara*. Leaving impressions is important because of the memory. If they didn't exist we wouldn't be able to remember anything, but the trouble lies here because we can't get rid of the memorized stuff so easily. That is, we are trying to do it in a wrong way. Remembering exists because of the finding sense, and not staying trapped inside with the ceaseless reliving the impressions.

Impressions are responsible for the mechanical repeating of the contents we used to experience. If some outer influence at one point led us to commit something negative spontaneously, if we remain equally unconscious and passive, we will only continue to repeat this evil act we have learnt to commit even when the outer influence is missing. That's why people commit so many evil deeds that can't be explained any other way but possession. If they were possessed the first time, they go on committing evil deeds because they think they were the ones who committed it the first time, they are unaware of the external influences and their own mechanicalness.

When our life and work is mechanical, then this mechanicalness extends to the mind to be formative as well, to think mechanically, to be the slave of impressions because he keeps repeating them and identifying with them. *Those impressions in us act as feedback like the informative fields for shaping the outer events.* This way we are caught in the chain of karma, action and reaction of our deeds and misdeeds.

When we break up the mechanicalness by introducing bigger and bigger consciousness and the ceasing of identification, then the impressions serve the purpose they are supposed to serve, as the means for memorizing so that the meaning of being in the body can be known and also our freedom, and not a bigger and bigger attachment. Using the same function we can be enslaved and we can set ourselves free.

With this knowing the work on oneself can start.

Work on ourselves starts when we realize that what we call karma is associated only with the external experiences and our vision of the body, that the soul is only the witness in the body and the most supreme attractor of all the experiences, all the outer events related to the body. All its karma is actually that what it itself attracts and the awaking experience of existing. Karma then stops and disappears. We have nothing more to attract into experience when we come to the subject of all the experiences, the one who attracts everything, the one who experiences karma. Karma exists only on the outside, while the mind is attached to the objects.

The moment the soul starts uplifting returning to itself, the Divine, to overcome the natural conditioning, that same moment nature starts transforming to the Divine. The shift of the consciousness happens then. Up until then only the external causal conditionality of the inorganic and organic world existed. It existed for as long as the soul was descending down to the organic world, gathering all the experience, getting attached to them. Only when the soul, after plenty of experiences, starts to release itself of the illusory identification with the objective world and starts to return to itself, to awaken, begins the creative transformation of the na-

155

ture to the Spirit, starts the true culture and civilization, the rule of heart and soul.

Until then the negative entities from the inorganic world rule together with their hybrids among people, in a destructive way. They broaden the specter of experiences of the souls to the negative, too, that souls themselves could never bring about, but the ones souls wouldn't want to cause, the ones they don't need. This is a universe where everything that could happen happens.

This world becomes a true human paradise only when the soul overcomes the identification with the body and the mind, and discovers its true nature. Only in such a way people become soulful and good, the way they are. All evil exists because people don't live in accordance with their own Divine nature. The answer has always been this simple.

32. SOUL AND SCIENCE

Everything a man does in every moment is some kind of nature transformation. Starting with thoughts being the finest vibrations of nature that resonate in the brain and the mind of man, he sees them as his own thoughts, and repeats them in a new way as his own. It designs what was, tests what is and plans how it could be. This way it designs the nature and events, makes new combinations, that wouldn't exist in nature if it weren't for the man, and his doing. Everything a man sees he designs, the external appearance he turns into information, into idea. And the reverse, he turns information into an external appearance, he materializes the ideas. This way man transforms the external and the internal. *Man through himself finalizes the process of the Divine manifestation, and with this finalizing expresses the Divine in the finest of ways, as love that understands everything and gives everything*.

Everything we see around ourselves man made with his own ten fingers. It has become what we can call the second nature, an artificial creation. This alienated, artificial nature, technology and civilization, has been putting the nature in jeopardy for a long time.

Why is it necessary for the nature to transform itself through the man and his work, with the presence of the consciousness of the soul?[46]

It needs to rise above itself to be able to be designed but also to be bridled in order for the man to set himself free. In the impersonal unity there is no consciousness of oneself, nor of the meaning. It exists only in the objective presenting. That is what the science if for. Science is a practical way of nature becoming aware externally. For as long as we are aware based on the potential of consciousness that the nature itself enables, and in unity with it, from the perspective of body and senses, mind and ego, we can't be objectively conscious. Objective consciousness is possible only with the transcendence of body and mind, overcoming the condi-

---

[46] A good answer to this question gave Hegel in the *Phenomenology of Spirit* with the story of master and servant. Consciousness (first as the slave) through hard work reaches itself, manifests itself, gets estranged only to find itself indirectly and become a master.

tions the very nature gives us. It is so because the objective consciousness arrives in nature, into the body, outside, it didn't originate from itself. All science is therefore a process of overcoming the nature, discovering that consciousness doesn't originate from the nature but consciousness enables the nature, that the entire nature is just an illusory game of consciousness, thus the awakening is all a man needs, and not any permanent identification with the nature, body and mind, or a continuous change of nature.

Besides making all natural processes objective and clear, science also increases the possibility of intervening in nature, therefore using science it can be discovered that nature is as constructive as destructive, that the nature isn't a basis of consciousness but the consciousness is basis for the nature – as the recent discovery of quantum physics and DNA show.

Actually, nature is neutral, destructive to the point we live our life the wrong way, and constructive as much as we respect and support it. Its destructiveness is a reflection of our lack of understanding nature, and the only correct understanding of the nature is possible with its transcendence in the consciousness, in awareness.

The whole nature seeks its outcome in the awaken man. For this reason man wanders, suffers and experiences destructiveness for as long as he is looking for his outcome in the nature.

The science will reach its creative peak when that is adequately comprehended, only then will science become positive and constructive. It will remain destructive until the primary significance is recognized and the role of the conscious subject, the key role being in the consciousness of man.

Science has come close to soul in the subatomic and cosmological research. Subatomic research has led us to pose a question of the influence of the subject on the physical phenomena, when it was noticed that a wave becomes a particle only during the presence of the conscious subject. A similar thing was discovered in cosmology, mainly that universe is the way it is because of the conscious subject.

The world doesn't exist without the subject who experiences it. This doesn't mean that world is an illusion, but it rather displays the sense and existential importance the subject has for the world. Namely, *the world exists to form a conscious subject.* Subject in the absolute sense is the Divine Absolute. In the area of the relative activity of nature he is the individual soul who as an observer through the man's open eyes gives to the world a testimony of existence. The more awake and open they are, the more the soul is consciously present. The whole nature exists for the observer. The observer whose sole purpose is to exist to serve the whole nature. Therefore, there are no fundamental differences between macro and microcosmic manifestation. It is one and the same event. Because of their unity, the subject and the world he is in are interactive.

The conscious subject is always on the boundary of micro and macrocosm.

Nowadays, in the many results from the area of cosmology, astrophysics and quantum theory, there has been discovered a whole series of amazing coincidences between the numeric values of some fundamental constants of nature ("the natural constants") for example, such as the ration between the proton mass and the electron mass. It has been observed that the very possibility of the existence of life depends on much of the congruence about to be discussed. It has been determined that certain characteristics of the universe have to be exactly the way they are in order for the evolution of a life based on carbon to take place (according to many people the only basis for a spontaneous origin of life) and in the final outcome – a man as the conscious observer. This fact being as obvious as it is led to the making of the cosmological theory of the Strong Anthropic Principle or SAP, which states that the visible characteristics of the universe, the way they are in it, are not a product of coincidence or the natural selection between multiple choices, but a consequence of quite a specific purpose: creating the conditions for the origin of the conscious subject. That principle says: "The universe must have such characteristics that permit the development of life in a certain stadium of its existence." From this we can conclude that universe was created with the goal of creation and survival of the observer, and those observers are necessary for the existence of the universe.

Strong anthropic principle says the nature exists exactly the way it is, and that it can't be any different, in order to create a conscious subject, that there would be no nature without the conscious subject. *It is primary. It projects the whole nature.* Soul we can understand as the absolute or the transcendental subject.

The purpose of subject, and its fundamental significance for the existence of the objects, will become clearer to us if we see that the light of one star, for example, would never have been spotted if it hadn't fallen on the retina of the observer's eye, the subject. It would spread on end into the void and there would be no purpose to its existence. Nothing exists in nature without meaning. Therefore, without the subject that is aware of their existence, the stars literally wouldn't exist. When the subject observes its light and becomes conscious, the spreading of the light achieved its purpose, it got the adequate reflection in the eye of the observer and the actualization of its purpose in his consciousness. All the objects find the meaning of existence in the conscious subject. Therefore, in the ancient science *sankhya,* it was said that the nature *prakrti*, serves the Spirit *purusha.*

Since the world exists only as an act of perception of the conscious subject, the world disappears for that subject when he is no longer aware, during the deep sleep without dreams.

Naturally the world exists during our sleep, Moon will exist even if we don't look at it, but that is because there are always conscious subjects somewhere in the universe, because the universe wouldn't exist without the conscious subjects.

Before people were so the conscious subjects were stars. They influenced the creation of matter in the form of planets on the cosmic plain. Planets then, as conscious subjects, influenced an even finer forming of matter into life energy, into all the living world on them, depending on its position and the connection with the other planets. The link between the micro and macrocosmic influences shows the science of astrology. In the end people as individual souls are the finest attractors that cause all the events we see as the world of human experience, technology, civilization and culture.

Before the stars, the Divine Absolute itself was a conscious subject. It is that now, too, it has just taken the finest individual personification as the human soul, the Self, the experience of "I am". For this reason the energy only in the presence of mind, under his influence, acts as matter and a special shape. Under this influence everything we see exists. That's why the mind affects the matter. That's why the law of attraction works. That's why all the enlightened ones say that cosmos is in us and that we are no different from God. An enlightened man is the God himself as the personality.

Cutting a long story short, a natural man, the way he was born, doesn't do anything, the nature does everything through his body and mind. The scientific development up till now has only increased the possibility of its unconscious action, which is as destructive as it is constructive. The only natural dialectics of opposites maintains the balance between the constructive and destructive effects of the scientific activity on the unconscious man. Our walk on the edge of self-destruction only Mother nature manages to keep in balance somehow, so life goes on.

Science is still compelled to operate on the physical plane only, with sufficient empirical experience which has been proven experimentally and is applicable to all the subjects. It is therefore required to negate the soul and the nature of consciousness which directly originates from the soul. The science of psychology deals with the awareness of the physical mind exclusively and with its psychodynamics. The very notion of the soul evades science and is reduced to certain foggy psychoenergetic phenomena of the body and mind, which appear and disappear together with the body. Hence, soul as the transcendental divine consciousness in man has not been recognized or welcomed by the science. However, science would be more consistent with its own method if it were at least open for the possibility of such an eventuality (were it to acknowledge Edmund Husserl). Unfortunately, there is a great tendency to overlook, even falsify, the whole issue of soul and consciousness. Science has of yet been unable to define consciousness. Consciousness is presented as a product of the unconscious matter, which is meaningless, just as a bunch of physical, sensory information that can be stored and transferred to a new body, and this is referred to as the soul. This ridiculous materialization of consciousnesses and a very defiant stance reveals a conspiracy against the consciousness and the soul in science, together with an attempt to conceal the truth of the higher dimensions. Perhaps the reason for this is the fact that science serves the interests of the corporations, the biggest one being the Military-industrial complex. They will undergo severe upheaval should people know the true nature of their soul, its divine origin, and once they get acquainted with the divine soul as the source of all the consciousness, and realize that there is not a multitude of consciousnesses, that it is one and the same throughout the entire existence, in all the people, in the same way that existence keeps uniting everything into one unison. How would people wage wars on one another if this were clear to all and proven scientifically?

Science will become as constructive and positive as the man is aware of himself as the soul, when scientists finally solve the problem of subject in themselves, and not outside in the theories. When they finally realize that they are those subjects they contemplate about and who have a crucial effect on the physical reality. Afterward, we will probably not find ourselves in such an absurd situation where physicists who act as wise guys while debating on the subject of physical reality, make atomic bombs, or inform us how we have 'proved' ourselves immature for a normal life on this planet and is, therefore, necessary for us to move to another planet (probably until we destroy that one as well) – instead of making life here better; or that it is necessary using: wars, vaccines, and poisons in the food (GMO) to reduce human population to half a billion – to make us easier for the violent control of the same heartless rulers who actually generate all the destructiveness in this world, among others such "scientists".

This self-knowledge is the oldest science in this world, the science of yoga and meditation, which can be found in "The Yoga Sutras" by Patanjali. Meditation is the only science of the future. It is a science of the soul with the practical implementation. Everything that could have been done externally, has already been done. Nature has finished its evolution by forming the human body and enabling the conscious subject, and the man's knowledge of the outside world is drawing to a close with the understanding of the DNA and the quantum field. The only other further evolution can be the inner evolution, man's self-knowledge. Only with its right development the outside world with the aid of science will become a heaven on earth.

33. SOUL AND RELIGION

The real religion is system of knowledge which should systematically guide the soul to a correct life and work while it is in the body, and to reach the self-knowledge.

Unfortunately, it hasn't been so for a long time now. Such real religion, which was the school of objective knowledge, existed only in the dawn of the human civilization on this planet, in the days before known history, when there was one human race from Ireland to Tibet, from Siberia to Egypt. It was broken up into many peoples and languages, its purest remains in the new history are known as the Ancient Slavs. All the members of the white race today originate from them.

In this original civilization all the ancient knowledge of the soul, of the Divine and the true nature of the man's life as the reflection of the Divine was saved. In the newer history, of about 10, 000 years ago, all the knowledge was saved in the old schools of knowing, which later came to be known as the Gnostic schools in the Near East, Sufi schools in the Middle East, and the schools of yoga in the Ind Valley, on Tibet and in northern India. Later, during the era of degradation, those schools became the monasteries of the closed type. One part of the objective knowledge from those monastery schools managed to find and convey to the modern man G. I. Gurdjieff.[47]

This original mankind and its ancient knowledge were gradually dispersed under the influence of time and the geographic separation and distance, because they didn't use technology. Likewise, under the influence of the inhuman hybrids who first conquered and destroyed ancient Summer of the old human civilization, and created Babylon, and from there on spread all over the world as the elite of rulers and priests that has been in power to this day. These hybrids have taken great care to eliminate any possible trace of the original human civilization and the ancient knowledge. All of the

---

[47] It is imperative for everyone to get to know the works of Gurdjieff and his disciples: P.D. Ouspensky ("The Fourth Way"), Rebecca Nottingham ("Fourth Way Teachings: Practical methods on Inner Transformation", "The Fourth Way and Esoteric Christianity), Maurice Nicole ("Psychological Commentaries on the Teaching of Gurdjieff and Ouspensky").

history we know actually consists of the systematic destruction of the ancient, true history of the humankind in this world. All of the known history is history of wars and conquests – all of which were completely unknown to people with the human soul in the olden days. Human hybrid rulers have taken on ancient knowledge and have been using it ever since to rule over people, to keep people in ignorance. All of the known history of culture and knowledge is in reality a systematic perverting of the true knowledge and culture. The essence of that knowledge of the human soul and the Divine has been perverted into the religions in existence today. What once upon a time used to be the school of objective knowledge and the practical implementation of this knowledge in a man's life, which consisted merely of the development of consciousness, was turned two thousand years ago into a mass mind control by means of religious worship of the abstract deity and the obedience to theocratic authorities.

The essence of the knowledge of soul and Divine has been totally twisted. The ancient knowledge referred to the Divine as the only and the greatest reality, and therefore there was no need to discuss or prove, let alone call upon or pray. There was no difference between the existence itself and the Divine, between a man's soul and the Divine. Traces that point to this unity can be found in Vedas and Upanishads. This unity was very skillfully thrown off its center with the teaching that man has to become one with the Divine, that he has been thrown out of paradise, that he is not in the unity with God, and that needs to return to paradise, but never concretely, always on the road to heaven, always waiting for God, hoping for him, and aspiring to him. In short, the knowledge of the original unity has been broken up into the mental projection of space and time. God has become a distant idol we need to aspire to and authority to be feared, and man thrown out of heaven and permanently sinful.

It was all depicted in the biblical myth of the snake (personification of the reptiloid) who talked a man into trying a mental projection, into distinguishing, as the only way to become one with God. In the very story the lie is obvious, because man had already been one with God because he was in heaven, and created in God's image. He was not meant to become. This is how a modern history of lies and deceit originated. But also the great process of awakening of man.

Nowadays the influence of the biblical snake, the reptilian hybrid, has been institutionalized as Vatican, which in translation means "the divine snake". The truth is not in hiding, although the people have been hypnotized into not seeing it, always trying to bite some bait, the apple of all kinds of knowledge and the passions of life.

In the East the knowledge of the unity of a man's soul, *atman,* and the Divine, *brahman,* was renewed very quickly in the works of Adi Shankara, but was deliberately warped in the endless philosophizing of the *advaita vedanta.* Very soon it was turned into speculative philosophy and abstraction, and drowned in the swamp of all possible demonic religious cults and sects that rule India today.

It has remained perfectly preserved in Buddhism, not as knowledge though, which can always change, but as practice which leads to true insight and knowing. That's why Buddhist teaching has always been persecuted and falsely interpreted, like today by the Jesuits who "translate" it into many world languages with the delicate twisting of the essential knowledge, so that it seems that Buddhism is a "religion without a soul", "the teaching of nothingness". Buddhism is just a practice of the man's awakening, nothing else. There is no teaching, it is not a religion. If the practice of awakening turns into a religion, then the dream continues. That is what the forces that keep a man in a dream did with the Buddhism. However the awakening of the soul is impossible to stop. That is how Nagarjuna came to clean up all religiousness from the practice of the awakening and to return Buddhism to what it originally is, and then Zen Buddhism and practice of *vipassana* meditations in Theravada countries and in the world, as a return to the original practice of awakening.

Therefore, we have the following situation today: on one side we have all the Judeo-Christian religions, Islam being one of them, that were created for the mass mind control, who only use the illusion of religiousness, religious terminology, because the mind must be attracted and deceived. This deception is made easy with the fact that man is a religious being essentially, because of his soul which is of Divine origin. In his unconscious state man projects his religiousness on the outside, because unconscious is projected outside, so he has always worshiped the Divine in everything, he would raise a stone and worship it. Inhuman forces that rule over people in this world use this in all ways: lead to the projection of the mind, to simulation and simulacrums of reality and religiousness.

It is all demonism basically which represents itself as the institutionalized religion.

On the other hand, we have a remnant of the ancient knowledge of the true relationship of man, his soul and the Divine, the teaching of the awakening.

The oldest remains of the ancient knowledge of awakening are in Jain religion. It is a path of the ascetic purification, which boils down to the total nonviolence and the dedication to the Absolute. Today this ancient knowledge has been lost even in Jainism by a banal imitation.

The purest theoretical postulate of the path of purification and the ancient knowledge has been saved in the teaching of *sankhya*.

Its practical implementation was saved in the work "The Yoga Sutras" by Patanjali.

A completely designed and practically implemented same path of purification and ancient knowledge was given to us by Buddha. Buddhism is the purest teaching and the most direct practice of awakening.

Other religions are mostly animistic, which means they either don't have a soul for the content or are degrading it to the animal nature. In such nations there is a belief that the soul after the death goes into the world of animals and demons.

The fundamental difference between the demonic religions that deceive the soul, and the path of purifying awakening of the soul is in the following:

The demonic religion always presents the Divine on the outside, as the God with a specific name, even shape, or without the shape but with a well formulated book which he dictated, as the heavenly authority forever unattainable to an ordinary mortal man, so nothing is left for man but to make some relationship with this authority, a vassal relationship of an obedient believer and to hope eternally for some external mercy and something better.

The teaching of awakening only enables the man to awaken to what he truly is as a soul, for the only, Divine reality, and therefore doesn't create any mental projections about reality, about the Divine, actually it annuls them all and gradually reduces in the man himself through the discipline of awareness. If the Divine absolute is the only reality then there is nothing there to think about, all thinking moves away from this reality, into an imaginary space and time, every presenting of reality annuls the very reality, because reality is always here and now. That's why it is the only reality.

Learning about awakening is a mental hygiene. It is completely based on the discipline of the being, on cleansing the mind of all deceptions so that reality can emerge through the mind, as it is, and not as it is imagined.

The second fundamental difference between the demonic religions that deceive the soul, and the path of purifying awakening of the soul, consists of affirmations and the negation of the very soul in the man, and its true nature.

The demonic religions teach that man is sinful and that he can't know all by himself the difference between the right and wrong, what is Divine, and what is not. That's why he needs a religious authority who will teach him that, and a man must accept that ethics and ideology to be as close to God as possible. This teaching takes place however only on the superficial part of the conscious mind, big part of the conscious mind doesn't change, and only repression is achieved through that, consciously man even tries to imitate the religious ethics, and unconsciously represses all the contradictions of the ethics in question. Hence the hypocrisy being the basic characteristic of believers of demonic religions, and crusades and bigotry toward those whose ethics doesn't comply with their own in some details, the divisions are the external reflection of this division in the people.

The doctrine of awakening teaches that only from one's own Self (Heart or Soul) man can know what is right and what is not. There is no other way. The knowledge of rightness depends on the man's relationship toward himself, toward the Self, from the purity and objectivity of his consciousness. Only then man can know the essence of all the ethics and the righteous living, straight from his soul. This essence then he manifests as the pure Good and Love. The maturity of the soul, that is the awareness of the Self, is the only one that decides on what and whether we will see and understand truthfully. Without that maturity we may be staring at the greatest wisdom and we will neither see nor understand anything. Or it may even seem foolish to us.

In order for this directness and the only correct bond with the soul be upset, and man made the slave of evil and all perversions (from sexual to ethical and metaphysical), religions with their ethics were created to impose from the outside as authority. The very idea that man himself in his soul knows what is right, was condemned as heresy with the dogma of the original impurity of man, by imposing guilt through the conviction that all the wrongdoings were committed by man and that is why he is sinful.

Any imposing of any kind of the Divine "truth" or "law" as instant spirituality has the only aim of repressing and deceiving a man's soul – although it is generally presented as useful teaching. Namely, the Divine is projected in the form of individual souls being able to know themselves in that role as well, as the individual being, of its own free will, where the individual with its own free will conform with the Divine, which is the only reality. Imposing authority everyone must submit to and ethics one has to imitate the free will of the individual is sabotaged in its efforts to conform to the Divine principle of its own will and following its conscious decision.

Judeo-Christianity is the leader of the sabotage, in it all human and everything regarding soul is repressed in the name of the imposed "law" and "God" – instead of being encouraged to develop and rise to the Divine.

Instead of the Divine being the secret that attracts in which the soul grows to its unutterable Divine essence, in demonic religions God is out in the open, and given to the full, he even dictated in one book everything a man should know and anyone who questions the superior authority is accused even murdered, like in Islam.[48]

---

[48] Orthodox religion should be distinguished from the Catholic and other Christian teaching here. Only the Orthodox religion has kept some of the real relationship toward the soul, of God as unutterable and unexpressed essence, of goodness and love which is shared equally with everyone on their way to God, but only in some old theological discourses. Today none of it exists in the

A true religion has no fetishes or laws, it is not written any-where because it is alive here and now, it is a constant growth in the Divine. The real religion manifests the Divine through man, it helps the man to manifest all the Divine blessings from his soul always in an individual and original way.

A false religion always imposes external God to the man, as su-preme authority, with the universal pattern and laws that apply to everyone, preventing the man to manifest any characteristics of its Divine soul in an individual way, that the freedom of its manifest-ing represents the only authority.

This prevention is the true goal of a false religion. Every false religion is mind programming and enslaving the people by some authority. False religion is every one that is institutionalized and imposes everything externally, for centuries it is the same and all people have to serve it instead of it serving the people.

The only true religiousness is the growth of the soul to the Di-vine, from conditionality to freedom, from the unconscious to the conscious.

That's why everything that is represented as religion, and con-sists of answers given to all the questions, menu, everyday con-duct, to the most abstract metaphysical questions of God and the world, and all religious practice which is learning all the answers by heart and then copied, to call upon the Divine with magical rituals in front of the altar – cannot be called a religion. It is pure mind programming. Everything that is learnt by heart and mim-icked is mind programming. It is a forced mechanism of main-taining the unconsciousness of the people.

There is an open question here whether such authority is needed for people to be more or less civilized. A better question still is who is systematically keeping a man in an unconscious and de-ranged state with religions like these. Therefore we have a situa-tion that the more the people are unconscious the more they will need a religion and authority to cultivate them. It is a reflection of the man's unconsciousness. Behind all the scenes there is an obvi-ous effort of keeping this unconsciousness as long as possible us-

---

Orthodox church because it never really fundamentally separated from the Catholic dogma which is completely based on fraud.

ing such religions, that a free man's awakening and free conscious growth isn't allowed. Therefore, we have two thousand years of unchanged state of spiritual darkness, and barely a few decades in the twentieth century when man reached for the stars, consolidated and designed all the knowledge from all the spiritual traditions. This unsteadiness of the development shows that man is capable of much faster development, and somebody is preventing and controlling that.

True religiousness is always personal and it spreads all by itself, from within, with the goodness of the soul itself, unobtrusive, it is never the same for everyone it rather always has a different face, a face of every man. It is completely realized only in an awakened man because it serves his awakening.

Any imposing of the ethics from the outside, in the dogmatic form which is learnt by heart and mimicked, splits the mind into being artificial and hypocritical and which manifests on the outside, and natural which is repressed. This schizophrenic mind splitting and repression create hypocrisy which is a characteristic of every believer. That's why there's a thin line that separates a religious fervor from the genocidal slaughter, and sometimes that line is missing. That's why all the religions and ethics haven't made a man any better. Quite the contrary. They were created to prevent the man from expressing and recognizing his innate goodness with the counter-effect of the story of the external God, and the imposing the dictatorship with the "God's laws". It comes as no surprise then that all the psychopaths, mass murders and terrorists call upon God and the quotes from the Bible and Koran as their inspiration, while at the same time the president of the country that starts all the wars swears on this same Bible.

Basic mechanism with which the authority of the artificial, external "God's law" is maintained is identification with the body and mind. The more we are identified with the mind the more we are alienated from the Divine reality, and separated from ourselves. It is absurd but true: the more we are identified with the body and mind the more split our mind is and the more we are alienated we are from ourselves. The more we are aware of ourselves as souls independent of the body and mind, the more whole we are, even the mind is more whole and the body healthier. Because of this identification reality always looks absurd to us.

Identification is maintained with the illusion that we do every-thing, even evil. Man's soul never does any evil. It actually never does anything, it is just a witness and as such it attracts all the events taking place. When we are more aware of us as soul then we are always positive and spontaneously attract/do good and right. When we are unconscious we are always identified with something and then the contents of that identification depends on what we are going to do, most often it is not good. Only when the soul is weak as a witness of our identification with something else, and the body it is in is possessed by the negative forces, then that body does evil. Soul is during that time pushed aside, mind isn't conscious, and indeed, after an evil act he always remembers that somebody else did it, that he was possessed, or he doesn't know what happened to him, he doesn't remember the act itself; he committed it in his moment of weakness.

Of course, we should be responsible with our body and do right by it, but we can never be and act while being identified with the body, but only through the knowing of our true nature which by far surpasses one individual body. With the ceasing of identification with the body, we know our true nature of the body and have ob-jective attitude toward it. It may seem paradoxal, but it is so be-cause the soul enables the body, not vice versa. Therefore, if we identify with the body, we are so unaware of the Divine Spirit which we are and we are so manipulated by the alien, negative forces, inorganic entities. *It is absolutely necessary for them that we feel responsible for what they have done to us, and through us. Otherwise they simply won't make it. It is necessary for them that we remain ignorant of the influences of other dimensions. Because if we don't know about them – we will blame ourselves through the identification with the body. This is how it works.*

That is one more deception of the demonic religions: they pro-ject all the higher dimensions, which are hidden away from the man's mind thanks to his senses while the man is in the body, somewhere outside, into space, to some imaginary heavens, into time, in the myths and legends when once upon a time the heavens were open to some special prophets. That is mystified with ritual and religious holidays. In every possible way the higher dimen-sions are hidden away from man, nobody states that he is made of them, like the microcosm.

These forces forbid us to think of our identification with the Divine, they teach us that this is "sinful", that that's exactly "what Satan wants" – for us to think we are God.

This, too, is identification with the body. Naturally, Divine isn't just this body-and-mind (Ego), it is infinitely bigger than it, this bigger we have in mind when we say we are Divine. Our soul is far bigger than our body, it doesn't die and it's not born with it. We are far bigger than this body. We only dream we are in it. When all the mystics and saints say we are one with God, they mean that they are not identified with the body and the bodily mind. They mean they don't have an Ego. Every guilt and being sinful and decline into identifying with the body and being unaware of its real, Divine nature.

The true nature of the man's soul is directly negated by the theses that people themselves are evil, that is advocated by the demonized people, the inorganic entities themselves who through them have a major influence on the education and knowledge. They impose the feeling of guilt on people with this, and a feeling of inferiority. They keep people in ignorance and paralyzed using this method, usually those who are incapable of resisting possession or mind programming. If people were aware of the Divine Grandeur of their soul they would get rid of their possession straight away. But they are, first through Judeo-Christian religions, made to believe that they mustn't identify with God in any way, that they can be in some relationship with God through church, of course not one with him, it's a heresy even to think such a thing – and then that they are to blame for all the misdeeds that exist. If devil is mentioned he is somewhere far away, as the enemy of God, in the imagination and fears, in order to intensify them. That's how people are captured, that's the real meaning of mind division.

The mind division is stimulated by religious teaching that contains open contradictions. Christianity is based on the teaching that God became the man in order to save the man, which would logically mean that with this act man becomes God at the same time in the act of salvation. But this idea of God knowledge, and the Divine nature of man is being negated strongly and forbidden to people. Moslems also brutally killed one of the greatest Sufi mystics, Mansur Al-Hallaj because he said "I am God" in the rapture of

God knowledge. It is true that there is a danger that the split mind or Ego starts imagining thing sand assigning itself Divine attributes, but these cases are so obviously psychotic that they can't be the reason to forbid the highest truth of the unity with the Divine. To be one with God means not to have an Ego. If Ego proclaims itself the God then it is insane. The difference between these two states is so huge and obvious that it can't be equated. But it is equated by those who fake everything.

True religion needs to teach the man how to consciously recognize its unity with Divine, because up until that point he was unaware of this unity. In the way they have taught him so far they only increase the psychotic identification with the mind and Ego, a conscious separation from the Divine.

34. THREE KINDS OF WORK: PHYSICAL, INTELLECTUAL AND INTENDING

In accordance with the manifestation of soul in the relative world, where it, although one with the Divine, shows itself in various modalities and states of the mind, as young, mature or fully mature, there are different ways of actions of the soul according to their manifestation.

The lowest form of manifestation is that of the young souls, which is the roughest and identified the most with the mind. Work and actions of such people are most dominantly aimed at physical labor and rough experiences, positive and negative. Those are the hardworking people that dig for ore from the depths of the earth to be able to build and shape everything we see as the attainments of civilization, who sow and reap the fruits of the earth to feed all the other people, who work hard while building with their own ten fingers the objects we live in. Although they are at the lowest place in this imaginary hierarchy, they are actually the carriers of everybody else, who would be completely unable of surviving several days without water, ready-made meals, technology and central heating.

Young souls are undergoing a training for the life in the physical world and therefore their experiences are rough and simple: good and evil, pleasure and pain, having and not having. They learn on their own skin the laws of existence and how to keep it with their own hands.

Their mechanicalness and susceptibility to the outside influences is the highest. Their mind is completely turned to the outside and all the inner activities, values and activities they see as mysterious or "Divine" activities and treat them in a magical way, with rituals and convictions, while on the outside they are rough materialists, they believe only what they can see with their own eyes and what they can do with their own bodies.

The following are the developed souls, who act on a higher level, their preoccupation isn't simple existential states, but their dramatization for the sake of creating. Those are the people who create higher values using their mind, they make all the heritage of culture and civilization, they design and experience all the possibilities of existence using everything that has already been made and constructed. They design the laws of existence from the past and try to implement them and improve nowadays world by reducing conditioning of the laws of existence and outside influence. Medium developed souls arrange outside life in order to reduce the forces of conditioning.

Their mind is still turned to the outside, and only temporarily becomes aware of the inner values, but in an abstract manner. That's why they most often deal with the outside world, and arranging environment and the conditions of life, and inner topics they approach philosophically and theoretically, lately psychologically, as well. This way they manage to overcome external influences partly and to rule themselves, at least in controlled conditions, to construct some culture and behavior and some kind of freedom of action.

The most advanced souls are the least present and their influence and work doesn't refer to this world and improving the conditions of living. Their world is maintaining the objective knowledge of the soul and Divine in the conditions of physical life. Their mind is completely aware of itself, they don't look for answers outside, nor do they deal with the outside conditions of life, but solely the arrangement of the mind itself and connecting mind with the soul. They do this in various ways, sometimes as teachers and saints who affect multitudes of people, sometimes as unknown people who individually help some advanced soul to develop. They are completely aware that all the higher dimensions are in man and that the Divine is the only reality, man's as well, they recognize all the outside illusions, therefore their entire lives can be brought down to the mental hygiene, and purifying the finest mental conditioning for the Divine reality to be able to shine through man's complete personality.

In reality, all souls do the same job: cleansing space for the presence of the Divine, its grounding and realizing itself here and now, through the life of man – but on varying levels. Young souls do it on the rough level, by dealing with the existence itself, the medium developed souls elaborate all options of existence on a higher level, partially outside and partially within the man, connecting the outer world with the man's inner world giving meaning to all the causes, and the most advanced souls this same cleansing perform in the finest of ways, at the very source of all deceptions, in the mind itself, by cleansing the mind of all contents.

The way everything in the relative world contains its opposition, the same way the opposition is at work here. Although the most advanced souls are above the identification with the body and mind, they are the most realistic, emotionally the most mature and existentially the most aware of all. Although young souls deal with the existence the most, they are the least aware of the real nature of existence. That's proof that only the presence of consciousness uplifts the man and releases him.

Young souls face all kinds of influence and conditioning and they try to reach the results of their work following the law of causality, attached only to the senses and matter, the subjective way of thinking, they can achieve only the quantity they are able to do with their own bodies. Since their mind is always turned to the outside, they see their obstacles toward the aim only outside and they put a lot of effort in removing the outer obstacles. This way they do the most physical work in this world.

Medium developed souls work on understanding the outer influences and their overcoming. They reach their aim and the results of work using their mind and knowledge, understanding the causes and predicting the consequences, perfecting themselves, planning and employing others to do the rough work in order for the aim to be achieved. Since they also follow causality, and that means they first have to provide the necessary conditions for achieving the aim, their results are partial, too, they can achieve to the degree of their planning of everything and removing obstacles. Since their mind is turned to the outside and partly to themselves, they still think that the chief obstacles are outside, but they know they have to adjust themselves to the goal, and succeed to the point of which they manage to change and perfect themselves. This way they do the most intellectual work in this world, collecting the most knowledge and information of the world, and the man's nature and development.

Advanced souls aren't identified with the body and mind, they don't work following causality or material conditions, and they achieve their results and goals by intending and attracting. They act with the consciousness which is outside the mind, meaning outside the time that exists only in the mind. Intuitively they know that reality is whole and out of time, that similar vibrations attract, and that everything is connected in the universe. That is why they consciously intend their aim and with the very intention attract it into realization, no matter of the current circumstances. They never remove the momentary circumstances first nor do they fight them, they don't provide the causes first, to come to the consequence, but they only intend the aim, the consequences, they just intend the aim, the consequence, as though it were done here and now, because they know that by mere attracting the aim all the necessary causes will be provided as well as the circumstances for them to be realized.

The most advanced souls with their own consciousness completely actualize the fact that everything exists because of the conscious subject, that the entire nature works for it. That's why they don't ask for anything and they don't work on the outside, they just attract everything that's needed with their intention to attract that. Because they don't have any desires for anything outside, everything that is needed comes to them spontaneously. The existence of any kind of desire for something manifests the attitude that they don't have that, and this attitude disables the having of that. The law of attraction always acts directly, like a mirror and based on the deeper conviction (we don't have something), and not based on the superficial mind that changes every moment (which wants to have something). Therefore, with wish for something we attract the situation we still don't have, and still want to have. If in the mirror of the Universal Field is our face that doesn't have and wants to have, that state will linger. The mirror of existence reflects everything, doesn't add anything new and doesn't take anything away, the point is just what image of ourselves we will project in it. Such an image we will receive back.

Advanced souls know that everything is in them, that all the higher dimensions are in the man, not outside of him, that everything takes place because of the conscious subject. Together with the attracting they in themselves enable the acceptance of what they intend in such a way that they remove all the obstacles in themselves, not on the outside. They know that soul is the most supreme attractor of all the events, and that exists in the body to experience certain things. They know that everything that is happening outside, around them, the reflection of the need of their soul to go through that, to be the witness of that; that they themselves attracted that into manifestation. Therefore, if you see a sick person nearby, or that someone behaves in a certain manner so that it negatively affects their life, they know that this scene (disease, conduct), was attracted by their soul because of the need for that experience, to be his witness. By bringing this process round, by understanding why this scene (a sick friend, a certain conduct) is happening before them, that is - to them, and thanking for the achieved event, they take it right to the end, to fulfillment. The friend is healthy again, the negative behavior changes. Unless, this disease and this conduct weren't part of their need for those experiences - it should be distinguished, if at all possible, if something is the need of the soul to experience, or to put others through it, because the souls are not here merely for themselves but for mutual purpose, and for others, to provide experiences for one another. Those are two types of soul work, for oneself and for other souls.

When a conscious subject experiences a certain phenomenon, it has reached its end, it doesn't have to manifest any more. With the conscious thanking and realizing that a certain phenomenon came about because of their attracting into experience (regardless of the reason, it may be for some karmic reason or just for learning), they annul the need in themselves for this phenomenon ever again taking place. Thanking with love this phenomenon that manifested in their experience, they return it to the universal Field everything belongs to. The feeling of gratitude and love is the emotional bond with the Field. It can't be experienced differently but through love and gratitude for enabling everything.[49]

It is the most supreme way of souls working on planet Earth.

Always when the mind is open for the presence of the consciousness of the soul, deeds and work are correct, supported by nature which in its entirety serves the Divine and his soul.

Always when the mind is closed to the influences of the soul, when it thinks that it independently owns the consciousness and the power of action, and when it tries to work, then this work is always more or less wrong, contrary to nature.

That's why one of the biggest Bringers of Light said: "But seek ye first the Kingdom of God, and his righteousness; and all these things shall be added unto you." (Matthew 6:25-33).

Since the whole nature works for the benefit of the Divine and soul, man shouldn't do anything of his own accord, intelligence and intention. He couldn't even if he wanted to. He would do the most and the best only when he turns to Himself, to his soul. Then everything will come to him in his best interest. Turning to oneself, one's own essence, is the point of all man's good deed in this world, all the culture and proper development of the surroundings. Man does right only by inaction. When he turns to himself, his soul, he has support of the whole nature. When he is turned to the outside in the illusion that he is separated from Divine Wholeness, then he goes against nature and that's why he feels suffering as impedance. Suffering is always the indicator that we are going against reality.

---

[49] This highest principle of work of the souls on earth is called *Ho'o ponopono*, a Hawaiian method of body and life healing. See more in the book "Zero Limits" by Joe Vitale and Ihaleakala Hew Len.

The entire process of the work of a soul is manifested in various ways as a measure in which the soul is present in the body and also a measure of the consciousness of one's higher dimensions. Young souls are those who have the smallest percentage of presence of the soul in their body, consequently the least presence of the objective consciousness of the higher dimensions, and the maximum influence of body and surroundings; medium developed increase their presence by increasing their consciousness and decreasing the influence of the body and surroundings, and the most advanced have gained the complete presence of the soul in the body.

The consciousness of the higher dimensions in the most mature souls is completely realized and effective: in the Air element their thought becomes Word or Logos, in the Fire element they use will or intention to realize thoughts, in the Water element they use emotion to shape and attract ideas, and they know how to realize everything concretely in the element of Earth. Immature souls don't have consciousness of the higher dimensions and that's why they act only according to the laws of lower dimensions, feelings (Water) and labor (Earth). The more the soul is mature in the body, the more it uses the laws of higher dimensions, of will and intellect (Water and Air). The most mature ones use only the presence of consciousness as intention, and space (Ether) enables it. Their consciousness is like space, it covers and enables everything that exists. Therefore, their consciousness is the same as that what enables everything.

It is wrong to get the impression that the most advanced souls achieve everything they want like magicians. Quite the contrary, they are the most modest and the most hardworking people, they adore physical work, making things, taking care of the environment, teaching others to work for the welfare of everyone. Their work isn't menial and exhausting like in the most immature people, but always voluntary and creative even when it is the most humble. They work always and tirelessly, there is no laziness in them, nor the selfish interests. They don't work so much for the aim but more because of work as the means of supporting life. In their work they are like the nature itself that does everything. Actually, they are aware of its work and their role as the witness and the most supreme attractor of nature's work, and that's why they participate in it willfully. Although, they know that they are the reason and purpose of the entire nature's shaping, they almost never attract results and goals to make work easier. It happens in their presence spontaneously only when it's necessary; suddenly the aim is realized in a miraculous way.

The most mature souls completely harmonize their intention with the intention of the Divine Absolute who, actually, is the only one that does everything. That shows the maturity of the mature souls, in knowing that Divine is in everything, in the conscious participation of it. This harmonizing happens automatically when the intention of the Divine is known. Then, it isn't possible to have any other intention, any will of one's own. Attitude "thy will be done" is insight into the knowledge that there is no other or a better will than the one of the Divine which enables everything. Any other will is only an illusion and dream, an error of perception or action. These mistakes constitute a man's life until he matures to the knowing of the Divine Absolute in him.

When the most advanced souls realize fully their presence in the body, they become those very rare cases when their body starts shining with the uncreated light.[50] Their work is only that: to be the light of work and of people.

---

[50] In the spiritual literature several of these examples were recorded, when saints turn into the light. We will name two, one from the earlier past and one more recent. The most well-known case from long time ago is by all means the situation when Jesus turned into the light on the mount Tabor, and a recent case is turning Bhagavan Sri Ramana Maharshi into the light during a meditation which was recorded by the baron Dr von Valtheim-Ostrau, whose writing presents Lama Anagarika Govinda in the book "Tibetan Mysticism": "An interesting description of this phenomenon is in the notes according to dates of baron dr von Valtheim-Ostrau, who was observing that in the presence of a modern saint, the last Ramana Maharshi of Tiruvannamalai. I translated the following chapter of the second notebook of his "Asian Diaries" called Der Atem Indiens (Classen Verlag, Hamburg 1955): "While my eyes were sinking into the golden depths of Maharshi's eyes, something happened, which I dare describe only with the utmost self-restraint and modesty, in the shortest and the simplest words truthfully. The dark color of his body was slowly turning into white. This white was getting brighter and brighter, like a light that was switched on in him and while I was trying to understand him consciously and with a clear thought, I immediately thought of suggestion, hypnosis, etc. That's why I was making certain "control checks" such as watching the clock, taking notes and reading, To this purpose I first put my glasses on etc. I was watching Maharshi then, who didn't turn his look away from me and with the same eyes, that were able to read notes in my diary, I saw him sitting on the tiger fur like a shining shape. It isn't easy to understand this condition, because it is so simple, so natural, so unproblematic. How I wish that in my hour of dying I remember it in full clarity!" (p.2461)

It is the light of our soul we see in the moment of dying of our physical body. The enlightened one is the one who does it consciously during his lifetime. Of the transformation of the physical body into the uncreated light, with numerous

35. WORK ON ONESELF

We had an illusion that we do something while the natural conditionality was doing it all, the same way we have an illusion that we are
setting ourselves free by some new work. Setting ourselves free starts
with inaction. With keeping still and numbness.

All events belong to nature or *prakrti.*

Soul is merely a witness of the events, consciousness is the one that
gives meaning to the happening.

Its differentiation is achieved only by the ceasing of identification
with events, not dreaming any more that soul is the one that works and
suffers consequences of this work, that the consciousness, which is
transcendental, changes and puts up with the changes of mind and
body, that it is no different from the content it illuminates. It is the
definition of the state of sleep.

The very presence of soul in the natural events starts all activities
and the entire existence: the very closeness of a conscious subject
moves the whole nature to shaping and action. The very action of nature dazzles the conscious witness to forget himself as the independent
and separated and to think that all the action is his, because he identifies himself with his thoughts, the finest vibrations of nature.

Human existence, like the place of the presence of witness and consciousness, represents oblivion and double confusion: on one side, the
very nearness of the witness and consciousness makes the nature seem
like it does everything by itself, and on the other hand a conscious witness forgets himself because of the proximity of nature, and identified
with it he thinks that he is the doer.

For the witness to free himself of oblivion and returned to himself,
he needn't do anything any more, he should just make the entire doing
of the nature that resides in the body aware in order to see that it is the
one doing everything, it breathes, it starts the heart beat, its finest frequencies, thoughts must be restrained with discipline and refrained

---

comparative examples from history within shamanic, religious and mystic traditions
see Mircea Eliade: *Mephistopheles and Androgyny.*

from any identification with anything outside, with anything at all, to be just he himself, to be able to know himself.

Such inaction and numbness doesn't present any avoidance of activities, quite the contrary, they are the fulfillment of the purpose of the entire existence of nature and all the activities, the attainment of its goal. Hence, the Divine completeness and ecstatic bliss during such inaction and numbness in which the soul of man awakens.

Such inaction in everyday action in Taoism is called *wu wei*, the practice of systematic appeasement is called *rupa-dhyanam* in the Buddhist meditation, and applying insight based on achieved appeasement and the transcendence of the mind is called *vipassana*. ***It is all the work a man needs in this world. Everything else is prolonging the slavery in dreams.***

The second and third sutra in Patanjali's "Yoga Sutras" say that the essence of yoga is in the appeasing the activities of the mind, then the witness resides in its essence, in itself.[51] The second saying explains the first: mind can never be appeased with its control, because it is part of the natural activity and it's not ours anyway. The mind is appeased with recognizing itself as a witness that is separate and independent of all the happening. Then the mind is calm because it doesn't affect the witness, us. We cease to attract the frequencies of nature, thoughts, to swarm in us looking for the meaning. The purpose has been achieved and sanctified. It also explains why thoughts can disappear in unconscious state, in mental stupor with insane people, or under the influence of drugs. They occasionally experience the absence of thoughts because they don't experience the awareness of the meaning of everything. Thoughts disappear for two reasons only: when they fulfill their purpose in designing and understanding (*prajna*), and when they don't have what to look for in a subject that has no objective presence of consciousness that would tie in a meaningful way the information of thought.

Only in a consciously realized total appeasement (*samadhi*) soul resides in itself, in its true nature, for the first time since it entered the physical body. The appeasement must be done in all the dimensions of the being, from the finest to the roughest activity: from the mind and

---

[51] Patanjali: *Yoga Sutras* I, 2: Yoga is the stoppage of the activities of mind. I, 3: Then the witness is established in itself. I, 4: In all the other states there is an identification with the modification of the mind.

performances, imagining and contemplating, feeling and emotions to the body and every movement of that body.

Those are the four foundations of mindfulness of Buddha's speech *Maha satipatthana sutta*. A thorough practice of the man's awakening is presented there. That speech together with the Patanjali's "Yoga Sutras" is the essence of the spiritual path of man and the practice of awakening of souls and the realization of the Divine in this world, and all the worlds. This practice is the only one that's right because it doesn't call upon the Divine and it doesn't call upon it from the perspective of the mind, but enables it to simply be, the way it is, by removing the mind, opening up space and creating void in the man's being, with the conscious permitting to be what had previously been unconscious, by numbing of everything that obstructs the consciousness of the Absolute to be here and now, by appeasing and numbing all the illusions that it's not here and now.

Work on oneself has the only goal of awakening or the self-knowledge.

The essence of the work on one's self is in the ceasing of identification of soul with everything it's not, and it's not anything but the Divine consciousness of itself.

The Divine reality is always one, but it has two aspects: either it is itself an Absolute, or it is an individual soul. Everything in between is an illusion. In this illusion is the entire cosmos and all our lives.

The process of awakening from that illusion isn't subjective, because the nature of the existing of soul in the body is reflection of the existence of the entire universe. The entire universe exists because of the oblivion of soul in the body, and the entire universe disappears with the awakening of soul in the Divine Absolute. It disappears because only then the Divine itself exists as the soul.

Soul already is in the Divine Absolute here and now, because nothing can be outside of the Divine Absolute. Everything that looks like outside and anything else is a dream.

Awakening is the disappearance of that dream.

It means that awakening is the disappearance of the illusion of existence the man himself.

It means that the reality here and now is such that everything else disappears.

There is no world in here and now. There is only the Divine. World exists only in the illusion of time and space.

36. MAN'S TESTIMONY OF THE PRESENCE OF THE DIVINE

Work on oneself is no different from life itself.

The entire human culture and life of every man are merely preparations for the final work on oneself, by gathering all the experiences for the consciousness of oneself. The consciousness of itself is the goal and purpose of human existence, every life and every life experience.

Work on oneself is merely finalizing that process in its realization and purpose.

Unlike the rest of the life process which was happening for the most part unconsciously and in a conditioned manner, and only partly conscious, work on oneself is a completely conscious process, so conscious that it doesn't deal with anything other than strengthening the consciousness as such. It doesn't change anything in life, it just becomes a conscious life, it just awakens life in all the details and aspects. If someone were to change anything in life, it would be some artificial work on oneself, it would be work on something else, not on oneself. Life and the work on oneself are one and the same thing, the difference is merely in consciousness and unconsciousness.

The unity of work on oneself and the life itself, the existence itself, rests on the unity of the Divine Absolute. It only exists. There is nothing else. The Divine Absolute is in the center of every shaping, in the foundation of every existence, in the heart of every being. That's why we say that the Divine Absolute is the witness of everything.

If a man is a microcosm, created in the image of God, then the Divine Absolute is a witness in man more clearly than in anything else.

Testifying presence of the Divine Absolute in man is the man's soul.

Consciousness in a man comes from the soul. Soul is our Self at the same time, our essence. Therefore, our consciousness is our essence, by awakening we become who we are, and awakening is the only "liberation of soul".

If the Strong Anthropic Principle (SAP) claims that cosmos the way it is exists with the purpose of creating the conscious subject; if experiments show that the conscious subject with his own existence influences the appearance and shaping of the matter; if Gnosticism and esoteric Christianity, and all the mystics claim that Divine through man continues its creation; if *sankhya* teaches that the entire nature exists to help set the spirit of man free – then the purpose of man isn't in anything outside, not in anything but to be who he is, to be the consciousness of itself. All the outside work was merely a preparation for the testimony. Testimony is non-work, the existence itself as consciousness-presence-bliss (*sat-chit-ananda*). Testifying is therefore the stoppage and numbness of every unconscious act of manifesting and looking for the meaning outside.[52]

That's why work on oneself, as the testimony that releases the presence of Divine, is something only the most mature souls are capable of, who radiate with Divine love and understanding of everything, who have undergone all the dramas of life experiences. To them the show is over, dream has been recognized as the dream, the moral and the contents of the drama have been understood. They can be recognized by their independence and the lack of attachment to life. For the testifying of the Divine are capable only the souls whose current incarnation is the last. If they have some more karmic ties and needs for experiences, testifying as the act of dedication to the Divine will be hard to do. Immature souls can't seem to be able to grasp the nature of testifying, let alone apply it practically. They still chase the horizon of their desires and illusions, but there is no horizon, the more we think we approach it the

---

[52] The essence of testifying and the meditative practice we are discussing here was elaborated in detail in my book "Meditation - First and Last Step - From Understanding to Practice". Buddhist literature that deals with the meditation is also a good source, *vipassana* and *satipatthana*. It is completely presented in the Buddha's *Great speech on the foundations of mindfulness* (*Mahasatipatthana sutta*). See the works of Yasutani Roshi for the *zazen* meditation *shikan taza*, as the most direct practice of testifying. His teachings of *zazen* meditation are in the book "Three Pillars of Zen" by Philip Kapleau, Anchor Books, New York, 1980.

more it keeps disappearing in the distance. Only when the desires go away, when the man looks into them and realizes that every desire is simply in vain, that it is a reflection of the unconsciousness, then he becomes helpless and without hope. But at that very moment turnover happens, a turnover starts to happen that had never happened in any of the previous lives, because it had been going in the opposite direction, toward the horizon of illusions.

In this disappearance of hope is the only hope, in this state of lacking any desires is the only chance for the man's fulfillment, in this huge helplessness, suddenly the Divine itself and the entire existence begins to help him. It is waiting. When it sees that man is acting in a self-willed manner, it doesn't interfere. It waits, it can wait forever, because to it there is no hurry. It is eternity. The moment the man isn't self-willed, the moment he falls, the moment he disappears, when he surrenders completely, like the dying man to an inevitable death, the entire existence comes rushing to him, enters him. And for the first time man's awakening starts to happen.

Due to the timeless essence of the soul, young and medium mature souls in the body can by working on themselves realize the testimony. Consciousness itself shortens the time of maturing. It is enough that with the right practice the presence of the consciousness is provided and it will speed up the time required for the maturing of soul. This way the practice of testifying is accessible to every man, the differences exist only in the detail that immature souls need more discipline and dedication to the teacher, and the teacher needs more patience with them, while the most mature souls need only to inform themselves about it and they will be able to realize everything.

We have said before that the entire process of the manifestation of the world happens as the fall or oblivion of consciousness from the Divine Absolute, that the manifested world is a manifestation of unconsciousness. Unconscious always automatically manifests on the outside as the physical world.[53]

---

[53] This truth is being deliberately hidden away from people in their education to make sure they are kept in an unconscious state. People are taught that unconscious is something imaginary and unknown, only psychotherapists can deal with, that it is a world of dreams, and that this physical world is real and only in it we are in a conscious state. The truth is quite the reverse: this what is unconscious for us is actually the Absolute reality, and here in physical reality

When the man is unconscious of himself as the soul, the Self or Divine Absolute, then it has experience of life in the world, body. This experience is therefore always connected with suffering. Suffering is always the illusion of separation from the Divine Absolute, from its essence. Suffering and destructiveness of life always increase when we look for the haven outside of us, in the change of the state of surroundings and the conditions of life. This painful quest is always a characteristic of immature souls, the entire human history and shaping of the world a man lives in, and all the maturing of the souls resulted in the knowledge that the salvation and the haven is in them, not in the change of outer states, that finding the real stronghold is in them, in the soul, and that's the only thing that can provide the real change of outer conditions.

Acquiring outer experiences was accompanied by the consciousness that the solution to human existence isn't in the outer adjusting, but these attempts have perfected the outer life, they have brought all the culture and science to man. The peak of culture and science will be in the knowledge that all the outer world is just a reflection of man's inner nature, that his DNA is communicating at the moment with the clusters of galaxies, that everything is contained in everything else according to the model of the holograph, that all exterior is man's interior.

This knowledge is the beginning of work on oneself or meditation.

That's why a man is appeased of all the outer activities and turns to himself: Because of the scientific knowledge that all the cells are conscious, that the entire life is a reflection of the consciousness, and that he is a conscious subject where the conscious existence reflects the best. That's why there's nothing for him to search for in the outside world. It can just turn to himself to be completely what he should be, what in reality he is. To finalize the sense of the manifestation of everything.

Since nothing exists outside the Divine Absolute, every conscious being that becomes fully aware of itself becomes the Divine Absolute himself.

Maybe the first thought that springs to mind is it's easy to say, but a completely another thing is to do it.

---

we live in a dream thinking we are awake.

The answer is the same: there's nothing else in the Divine Absolute.

Realizing the Divine is the easiest thing in the world, because that's what we already are. There's nothing else we can be. Any suffering and disharmony in our life happens because of the blind attempts to be what we are not. For the same reason all difficulties occur because we want to be something we are not.

Naturally, we are now unaware of our Divine essence. That's the only difference between us and Divine. The difference is always in the mind, in consciousness and unconsciousness. It is never in existence which is always whole because it is Divine. Only the mind gives us the illusion that we are separate from the Divine, that we are something other than what we are.

Our pure existence is in the Divine. In it we are unaware during deep sleep or aware during meditation. Then we are without the mind in both cases, in deep sleep we are unaware of it, and during meditation we are aware of it. That's why meditation means staying relaxed like in deep sleep, but still awake. The consciousness is present, but the thoughts are gone. It is the most natural and the easiest thing, because it refers to the pure existence such as it is, but we are accustomed to unnatural and phony existence. Illusions create all the difficulties in connection with reality.

The difference between conscious and unconscious presence in reality rests only on the focusing of attention, in the culture of attention, if it's turned to the outside in identification with the objects that it had projected itself, or it's aware of itself as the consciousness.

The essence of awakening of soul is being able to distinguish the consciousness itself from the contents of the consciousness.

The essence of unconsciousness is in the spontaneous reacting to objects and contents.

The essence of meditation is the same like the essence of realizing the soul. In meditation it is repeated on a smaller scale what the soul has to go through in all the incarnations, through death and being born: it gains the consciousness of its independence of the body and mind, of the projection of the outer world and unconscious responses to experiences we had projected ourselves. In meditation we die for all illusions of body and mind and resurrect as the soul in the highest heaven. Only that is the right meditation that leads us through death and resurrection. Everything else is the refining of an illusion.

The beginning of awakening is the ceasing of a spontaneous and programmed reacting of the consciousness to contents and in objective understanding that it creates everything by itself, attracts and shapes. It is a process of purification which is because of the experience of embodiment *experienced as separation from the body, from the feelings, from the thoughts and the mind – due to the prior identification* which had the shape of the body, feelings, and mind. Since only the whole exists as the holograph, there is nothing that can be separated from anything. The feeling of separation exists for the reason of identification, the ceasing of identification is experienced as separation. With the stoppage of reacting of the consciousness to its own content stops the further identification and the chain of the entire conditioned and painful wandering through the world. The consciousness as such remains, as the Divine Presence.

If we remind ourselves of the proof from experimental physics that man as a conscious subject is the fundamental cause for the pure energy to form into visible matter, for all the visible matter forms for him as the conscious subject, then the process of this separating purification in meditation will be all the more clear to us.

When a man knows these facts he is left with absolutely nothing but to realize that all the nature doesn't form for him alone, but for the Divine Absolute which is in him. That he himself was formed because of the Divine Absolute in him. Nothing else remains for him but to appease with his whole being, from body to the highest mind, in order to enable the purity of his presence through himself.

The ancient science of the Divine in man, *sankhya* and *yoga*, the purity of this separating presence of the Divine in man called *kaivalya*.

The word *kaivalya* denotes the state of that what is simple, not mixed with anything, authentic, pure, therefore, it contains the idea of perfection to the full. That's why it's used to denote perfection of the purification of the man's soul with its separation of everything that's not authentic. In this sense this word means the separation and secession of man's essence, soul, from the transient being in time, man's resurrection from mortal into immortal and un-born, from non-existence to existence.

The experience of detachment exists merely as the contrast to the former state of identification. In the whole which is the Divine Absolute nothing can be detached from anything. This only the awakened knows after the ceasing of unconscious identification and conscious detachment. If he hadn't been unconscious he wouldn't have needed awakening, if he hadn't been identified he wouldn't have needed detachment from the identification. And only after that, after the conscious detachment and awakening, man begins to take part in life and existence fully and truly, to be what he always is, to recognize it and love the way it is, because up to that point Ego-mind was separating him from the Divine whole-ness. That way the detachment of *kaivalya* is a paradoxal process of merging with the whole.

The experience of detachment exists for numerous reasons, one of them being the fact that soul in a man is a transcendental wit-ness, it was never in unity with the body, or the mind, it never really was completely one with any of the experiences that man has ever lived. It was always just a silent, transcendental witness of events.

The very presence of that witness attracted and created all the events. On the local level it attracted and created the events of his destiny, and on the global scale the events of the cosmos itself.

That's why the awakening of man is just a process of recogniz-ing this separate witness.

The witness is detached, there's no need to detach it. The prob-lem has always been that we were unconsciously attaching him to all sorts of things.

According to the most accurate description of the direct realiza-tion, the Buddha's words, this detachment is specifically experi-enced as insight: "This is not me" and "That's not mine", as op-posed to all constituents of the being: opposed to the body, feel-ings, the state of mind and every thought. Since it is not our trait and all the insight boils down to recognizing this simple fact, it is practically achieved with being still only. ***Kaivalya is achieved with being still only. In the mental quiescence everything that is not our authenticity is exposed and separates all by itself, every-thing that hides away our soul.*** However, because of the influence of illusions for such quiescence it takes the most supreme discipline, which requires the most supreme understanding.

There is no purification and liberation without the understanding of the affective tying in all the dimensions of being. The way the knot was tied the same way it has to be untied. It is the only way, because we have already said that the consciousness all by itself, under the influence of the mental patterns, projects its contents with which it identifies like in a dream. That's why it, and it alone can stop doing it when it realizes what it does.

Wakefulness is the presence of the consciousness in the being itself. Since the being is already energy which is aware of itself, man's wakefulness is nothing but a relaxed permission that it can, too, be that through his living experience, allowing universe to be aware of itself through man.

The essence of the spiritual liberation or awakening is in a real, authentic relationship of the man's soul toward existence whilst in the man's body. When there is a true relationship between them, a recognizing of the pristine independence of soul from the external existence. A man with his wakefulness corrects this relationship and puts it right. The external existence is not a problem, but being oblivious of its reality by the unawake man, that it exists only as the mirror of the self-knowledge of the soul, and via it the very Divine Absolute.

Independence of his soul man should, by no means, achieve and create, because it has existed forever, he should just recognize it perfectly consciously observing the very existence in which it mirrors itself. When the overall existence and all life recognize its reflection, only then will they know themselves. The whole mirror of nature is reflecting only him, his soul in everything, down to the last particle, through all the living beings to space in which all the galaxies are. They are all different proportions, dimensions and shaping of his soul.[54]

---

[54] *Isa Upanisad* (5-8): "That moves and That moves not. That is far and the same is near. That is within all this and That also is outside all this. But he who sees everywhere the Self in all existences in the Self, shrinks not thereafter from aught. He in whom it is the Self-Being that has become all existence that are Becomings, for he has perfect knowledge, how shall he be deluded, whence shall he have grief who sees everywhere oneness? It is He that has gone abroad – That which is bright, bodi-less, without scar or imperfection, without sinews,

Wakefulness is strengthened only by consistent presence in all the events and dimensions of existence.

We have already seen how all the dimensions of nature are expressed. Their vibrations create various density of events and the speed of time that shape the entire cosmos. They are microcosmically condensed in a human body in such a way that they constitute his physical body (earth), feelings (water), the general state of mind (fire) and every thought (air). *Of all the dimensions of cosmos the man, too, is made of, and consequently, he must stabilize his awareness with them, not the other way round. Therefore, he must strengthen his awareness in four ways: in connection with the (1) body, (2) feelings, (3), general states of mind, and (4) every thought.* Those are the four foundations on which the attention must be consistently collected and consolidated in the understanding of each one individually.

Man's life is unconscious and off-balance on such a large scale that he fails to see what determines and constitutes him, he almost never distinguishes the nature of his mental attitude from the feelings and the physical state and movement, and when he does so, it is temporary and without a permanent establishing. Interdependence of these makers conditions the consciousness to regard itself identical with them and the contents of their experience of the world.

All four dimensions of strengthening the insight represent a progressive cleansing of the consciousness from various kinds of fictitious contents and delusions, and its training to enable it to become one with the soul the way it really is.

The way that parent experiences maturing of his child, the same way man in this practice perceives his psychophysical being as it is and with this transforms it to the spiritual maturity. And with this act he transforms the outside world leading it to a higher perfection.

---

pure, unpierced by evil. The Seer, the Thinker, the One who becomes everywhere, the Self-existent has ordered objects perfectly according to their nature from years sempiternal."

Darsana Upanishad: "When all the beings we see only in our own Self (soul), and in all the beings Self (soul), then Brahman (Divine) we reach." X, 10.

The path of cleansing has two principles only: 1) A systematic observation of all the happenings in the body, feelings, mind and the contents of the mind – especially the feelings that accompany the remaining three happenings. 2) Lack of reaction to these events by getting attached, being repulsive or oblivious, and holding on to the indifferent establishing things as they are.

Both boil down to establishing, to constant neutral establishing of absolutely everything in us.

All beings react to events and by doing so they get involved and start living in slavery. The path of freedom is to see events for what they truly are, and when that's done properly, then the man is released from the spontaneous reacting to all the impressions (*samskare*) that they provoke, because he sees that it's not him, nor is that his. That's a characteristic of manifested nature, and not his soul. ***Everything a man objectively awakens, he sees that it's not his.*** He has always been free from the start, his essence is pure consciousness already, and in order to be what he is, he should just awake the happenings and stop, due to the identification with it, reacting blindly to its conditioning. For unconscious reaction to already existing events cause new ones, and that's how the chain of conditionality is created.[55] ***Only when it gets rid of the blind reaction, man's mind begins to reflect the soul, to act consciously and spontaneously in accordance with the Divine that contains everything within.***

However, independence of the objects, the contents of consciousness and outer influences is only one side of the medal. Above all, it is development and acquiring one's authenticity, the transcendental Self. The other side of the medal would be better and more conscious taking part in events, timely and creatively. Those two go together, automatically. One without the other does not exist. The independence of the Self we can achieve for one purpose only and that is to be able to perceive objectively all our existence, which is impossible to do while being involved in any

---

[55] That is the whole chain of man's slavery in which the forces that condition him also keep him enslaved. They program him to react always, constantly increasing his reactions and giving him false solutions to his problems that originate this way. He is kept in a closed circle. The only way out from the magic circle is his stopping, numbness. Never the modifications within the circling.

kind of identification. If all one can achieve is to be independent, then one slips into alienation and that wouldn't be right, the same way identification with the events wouldn't be. *A confirmation of the real authenticity of the Self is in adequate reaction and participation in the events, as well as his independence of all the events.* Besides, meditation is practiced in order to achieve better and more objective knowledge of events, and not to run away from them.

The power of distinguishing is developed and strengthened with meditation which is nothing but the effort and practice that enables better perception of activities of being on a deeper and finer level, before they are manifested in a rough way, the way we perceive with our senses and mind. When the deepest and finest possible perception of the being is realized, and that is the formation of thoughts as the most delicate movement of the being, then the observer resides in himself, man achieves self-consciousness or awareness. The consciousness purified like this automatically brings the saving distinction of the soul.

The contemplative practice, the principles of which have been introduced here, represents the man's first real turnover toward the spiritual freedom and awakening, to the life-saving differentiation of soul and existence, with which they are both realized in their essence. Absolutely everything a man was doing prior to this practice was referring to the experience of existing in nature and the karmic maturing in it. With this practice he for the first time in his karmic evolution truly turns the attention to himself or his authenticity, to his soul. Cherishing such attention, turned to oneself, where he matures as the independent soul, is what makes him free, always aware and truly endless. Nothing else.

According to Buddha's words: "In this limited body, no bigger than a handrail, the whole world is contained, the appearance of the world, the outcome of the world and the path that leads to the outcome of the world" (*Anguttara-nikaya*, 4,45). In a man who is meditating the outcome of the world is finalized.

The key to liberation is in the complete awakening of existence, in all its dimensions (body, feelings, the general states of mind and every thought). If we overlook one dimension, its unaware events will be the cause of our suffering and the feeling of enslavement. If we stress only one, for example mental (doing some meditative 'technique', a prayer or repeating *mantra)*, no matter what experiences and insights we had, we will always fall over and over again down to the lower states pulled by the weight of the remainder of the unaware existence, and we will forever repeat this one-sided practice hoping to reach a permanent higher state if we only repeat it often enough.

Besides the complete awakening of existence, the key to liberation is contained in the first principle of nature that it serves the purpose as reflection of the Divine, and in its finest aspect this mirroring can be brought down to self-knowledge and the liberation of soul. Therefore, a man doesn't have to do anything to know and liberate the soul, he should just be what he is, he should be still, he shouldn't move with the movement and events of nature, he shouldn't identify and react blindly and automatically with it, he should avoid getting attached with his own reactions. *When the nature is objectively recognized as nature, then the liberation of the soul happens.*

This liberating principle of existence is contained in all the real doctrines of awakening. In Taoism it is said that turbid water clears by itself when we leave it alone, when we don't stir it. Zen says that in quiescence of the body and mind, in *zazen* meditation, impure thoughts disappear all by themselves, and man knows his image he had had before he was born. In Patanjali's *Yoga Sutras* the whole yoga is defined as the appeasement of the activities of mind; then the observer is in its real, transcendental nature (Y.S. I, 2-3). The essence of Buddhism is in meditative, mental quiescence, attaining the objective consciousness in this quiescence and its application in all the other events and impressions (*vipassana).* The other true mystical experiences and the devotion to the Divine are based on this principle.

Soul is basically free already. If it weren't free it could never be able to be free, because if it didn't have the potential for it in itself, it could never become it. Everything is just transiting from the potential to real.

Having applied on himself the testimony of the presence of his own soul to the complete cleansing in the body, with all his feelings and thoughts, man becomes the witness of the Divine, he becomes his living presence.

Soul has always been just a silent, transcendental witness of the events.

The very presence of this witness has attracted and created these events. On the local level it attracted and created the events of his destiny, and on the global level the events of the entire cosmos.

That's why the awakening of man is a process of recognizing this separate witness.

He is already separate, there's no need for separation. The problem is that we have unconsciously associated it with all sorts of things. When there is no identification there is no movement of the soul. There's no time in which it was something other than itself, it is always present in itself.

Soul in awareness, in itself, reveals as immobile, only the illusion of the manifested world was revolving around it and shaping all its experiences known as lives and destinies. It itself was never going through lives, lives were going around it, like dreams. Soul was never doing anything, everything was being done for it.

Only with a whole and awakened soul one can see that the circle of the wholeness of the Divine manifestation has no beginning and no end, that it doesn't consist of opposing points, of the descending and ascending process, but that the Divine is equally present in every point of existence, that it is always and in everything perfect and complete. Therefore in the pure consciousness that mimics the whole there is neither development nor manifestation of the world. There is just the Divine presence here and now.

While the man was unconscious, he was dreaming that all the events had an effect on his soul, that it conformed to these illusory events and took part in them which created all the illusory suffering, wounds and scars.

In the awakened man the situation is quite the opposite: all the events conform to his soul and whatever the shape or state, they are as perfect as itself, as the reflection of the Divine Absolute.

Man's awareness is no different than the presence of reality itself.

Only with an awakened man, world becomes Divine presence and perfection.

The Divine that enables the world, manifests as awareness in man – and not as something of this world. It takes the image of man and then it works through him as pure love that enables everything.

Only an awakened man participates in the Divine presence and freedom that enables the world at every moment, because only through him this freedom manifests directly.

Only an awakened man contributes to the creation of the free world and takes part in its life for the benefit of all beings.

Made in United States
North Haven, CT
30 August 2023

40932846R00114